ON MILK
AND HONEY

ON MILK AND HONEY

HOW GOD'S GOODNESS SHOWS UP IN UNEXPECTED PLACES

Morgan Cheek

ISBN: 0692448756
ISBN 13: 9780692448755

DEDICATION

"And he is before all things, and in him all things hold together."

—COLOSSIANS 1:17

May this sacrifice of praise be pleasing to You, my Lord.

ACKNOWLEDGMENTS

To the many who have prayed for our family, brought meals, helped financially, cried with us, laughed with us, celebrated with us, listened to us, and simply stuck it out with us on our longest days-thank you.

To the physicians who seek out information and continue to research on behalf of our girls-thank you.

To the physical, occupational, and speech therapists who "play" with our girls, truly see our girls, and bring lots of enjoyment to our days-thank you.

Stephanie, thanks for believing in God's message in our family and continuing to love on our girls, keep me sane, and encourage me to use the gifts God has given me.

Sister, your listening and constant loving continues to serve a huge role in my heart and spiritual well-being, even from "afar." I love you and appreciate you more than you know.

Mom and Dad: Dad, you have allowed Mom to come be our "helper" during our times of greatest need; and haven't complained about it once. You have supported us both emotionally and financially and done it with joy. Mom, you have served tirelessly by our side since the day the girls were born. You love them, you know them, and you have been a source of reprieve for me on the weariest of days. You both have always been my greatest cheerleaders. Thank you doesn't seem like enough. I love both of you dearly.

Ally and Bailey Grace- you girls cannot possibly know the impact you are making on the kingdom. Your crowns will be full in heaven, and I love you more than words could ever express. You are fearfully and wonderfully made and have given Mommy and Daddy more joy than we could imagine.

Hugh, you may be behind the scenes in this venture, but you have patiently served me as I prayed, wrote, and pondered the words of this book. You are one of the most patient, loyal men I have ever come across; and I am humbled to be your wife. I love you!

My God, my Savior, and the Spirit within: May all these words be pleasing to You. I owe my very breath-my soul-to Your love. I have nothing to offer You but that which You have already given me. May this small book work for Your kingdom in a mighty way, all through Christ alone. Thank You for being strong in my weakness.

EPIGRAPH

"Peace is not a feeling in our flesh; it's a Being in our soul. It is not an emotion that comes around when all is well; it is God Himself penetrating His knowledge, His wisdom, His foresight, into the depths of who we are at all times, in all things."

—MORGAN CHEEK, AUTHOR

CONTENTS

FOREWORD

WHEN I FIRST MET MORGAN on the campus of the University of Georgia, I was struck by her beauty, grace, and easy demeanor. Then, she smiled. I was hooked. It is worth pointing out that this was at the end of a Special Olympics volunteer meeting, of which Morgan and I both were involved in. Irony simply doesn't exist. If irony did exist, I would be calling a sovereign God a liar. Our Maker knew exactly what He was preparing us for, as the pages ahead will reveal. I asked a friend at the time, "Where are girls like that hiding on this campus?" Since this time, Morgan has done anything but hide. She faces life with the most authentic, boldness of living out the gospel of Jesus Christ of anyone I know. In fact, some of the time it makes people uncomfortable. It makes *me* uncomfortable. The good kind of uncomfortable, for example, when you know you have just been given truth that may have not have been what you wanted to hear, but what you needed to hear. The one true God tends to mold us in this way. Chipping, sanding, grinding, smoothing, until we begin to bear His image. What a pleasure it is to see God forming my wife in this way.

God has given her a gift. A gift of the pen. She writes pages in minutes that would take most hours. Only the Holy Spirit outflow in her could achieve such tasks. A true hero of sorts. This might be a good time to praise other parents and caregivers of kids with special needs as well. What discipline, endurance, patience, strength, and sacrifice you show. In our home, I watch my wife give to our family day after day, with no time for herself. What is given in return? She would tell you that she deserves nothing. What *has* been given to her in return is the glory that lies ahead. She draws strength from the grace that Jesus gave us when He, Himself poured out on the cross, and this is all she needs. After all, the story of our daughters is as He designed it. Morgan and I know that Lord leaves nothing to chance, but all of creation points to ultimate plan of God bringing people to Himself through the redeeming work of His son.

In the pages of *On Milk and Honey*, you might see the heart of a mother; but it is truly the truth of God the Father. I am the father of our twins, but am in no real control. If we were in control, we would have written our story differently. Morgan's words tell the story of a God who allows suffering, even ordains it, but delivers mercy and cares deeply. Some things can only be answered by faith. I shudder to think of the reality of not believing this truth; to be left in a grave, downward spiral of despair. Morgan lives out the scriptures, "I want to know Christ and the power of his resurrection and the fellowship of **sharing in his sufferings**, becoming like him in his death, and somehow to attain to the resurrection from the dead (Philippians 3:10)." Morgan desires for you to see that beauty in what God has made in us, through us. We do take time to focus on the suffering, but only to highlight the One who suffered for us all.

My wife and I began our dating relationship around the words in Jeremiah 29:11. "For I know that plans I have for you, plans to prosper you and not to harm you, plans to give you a hope and a future." These words were delivered to Israel during a time of exile, oppression, hardship. This is not the prosperity gospel, just prosperity in promise. Morgan doesn't ask for pity. She wants you to see the sustenance of provision. I am honored to be married to her, and I am honored that *On Milk and Honey* shares the true message of hope in a world of uncertainty; a world in which you are offered temporary relief, while avoiding the reality of the pain. I pray that the Glory of God be revealed through this book in the way that Morgan reveals Him to me each day.

-Hugh

PREFACE

I HAVE ENJOYED WRITING AND speaking for as long as I can remember. I had a journal as an elementary student in which I would write eloquent details of the day and other musings of a sheltered, prepubescent little girl. I even won the state 4-H speaking contest in the fifth grade! (You will never find this on my resume, just for the record.) In all seriousness, writing comes as naturally to me as breathing. For several years, I contemplated how I would use this gift, and as life moved forward, I chose a career path that included a lot of documentation but not a lot of creative penning. And then, our twin daughters were born.

Bailey Grace and Ally Ruth, like most people's children, stole the hearts of my husband and me from the second we knew they had been entrusted to us. I never quite anticipated that we would have a child with special needs, much less two, but isn't that the way God usually works? He doesn't tend to do things the way I imagine them, yet He always exceeds my visions and rocks my world with His plans.

After writing a blog (hishandshisfeethisheart.com) for a little over six months, and God using it in the lives of many, He made it clear to me that a book was to be written. Many people have asked how in the world a mom with two kids with special needs had time to write a book. Here is my short answer:

God did it; and He did it in two days.

Before you close this book, now thoroughly suspicious of its contents, I urge you to hear me say that I truly believe He has something to say to you through our little family's story. I want you to know that I am praying that there isn't a single reader who would pick up this book, find a second or two of inspiration, think Hugh and I are "good" people, and then move on. No. If you did this, you would be missing the very meat of the story. (And you might get to know that Hugh and I at some point, see our sin and brokenness and throw away the "good" part altogether—whatever "good" means!) You see, the details God is writing on Ally and Bailey Grace, while unique and unexpected, are not the point of this book at all. These pages are written by a sinner, saved by grace alone, who has found God most strong in her own weakness. Within these pages is a story of His goodness that has shown up in some of the hardest days of my life. His faithfulness has been poured out all around us; and Hugh and I truly believe that no matter what "your" story is, He can be sovereignly trusted. To ensure that you see Him and not us, I have included a few questions at the end of the chapters, entitled, "Lessons Learned." These are only a guide, but please feel free to use them in whatever setting you see fit. I do believe that lessons are learned most abundantly in community, and I would love it if you read this alongside a friend or small group. That being said, if God has placed *On Milk and Honey* in your hands, my ultimate prayer is that you would know more of Him and His goodness and grace in all things by the time you are finished reading. I pray that He uses its contents to speak truth to you. I long for you to know that if He allows something in your life, He wants to use it for His glory and your good— truly and wholly. May this God, the God who is The Answer to each and every mystery, be your Rock today and always.

INTRODUCTION

IT HAS ALWAYS MADE SENSE to me that God appeared to Moses in the ways that He did. First, in Exodus 3:2, the Lord appears to Moses out of a burning bush. Later on, God calls out to Moses from the midst of a cloud (Exodus 24:16). This has been the story of my life as well. God, in His awesome, mysterious glory, shows up in some of the most real ways in the trenches of the unexpected. He often chooses to speak to us through the very things that perplex us. Exodus 3:7–8 reads as follows:

> Then the Lord said, "I have surely seen the affliction of my people who are in Egypt and have heard their cry because of their task makers. I know their sufferings, and I have come down to deliver them out of the hand of the Egyptians and to bring them up out of that land to a good and broad land, **a land flowing with milk and honey,** to the place of the Canaanites, the Hittites, the Amorites, the Perizzites, the Hivites, and the Jebusites (emphasis mine).

Now, if you continue reading, the lands that God takes the Israelites to don't always appear to be their anticipated provision. Furthermore, reading through the Israelites' always-swaying emotions is like riding a roller coaster; one second, they affirm that, yes, God has brought them to a land of milk and honey (Numbers 13:27). The next, they cry out to the Lord, saying, "You haven't brought us to a place of milk and honey" (Numbers 16:14). Oh, how I can relate. As you read through our family's story, you will find bits and pieces of those before us mixed in throughout. Our journey with Bailey Grace and Ally has been one in which I, like Jacob, have wrestled with God and His plans. I have doubted God's goodness and found myself bitter. One moment, I have praised Him; the next, I have been suspicious of His plans.

God's word uses the phrase, "milk and honey" twenty-four times. According to several sources, while many might think a land flowing with milk and honey refers to a prosperous, comfortable place, the combination of those two words is actually something more. Honey comes from a non-kosher insect, and milk comes from an animal of which many of the Israelites did not eat. That being said, let it be known that when God tells us He promises to bring us to a land flowing with milk and honey, we should expect the unexpected. Beyond that, twice in the Bible (Joshua 5:6 and Ezekiel 20:6, 15), it seems as if the land of milk and honey goes beyond this earth and onto the Promised Land, our heavenly home.

There has not been a season of my life in which things turned out the way I thought they would or even the way I would have determined. This season of parenthood in particular has rocked all my former expectations to the core and has caused me to dig deeper into God's Word and His promises more than ever before. I have found that in the way God says that He knows us through and through (Psalm 139:1), He equally knows our sufferings (Exodus 3:7). I have also seen that while I would not have chosen this story myself, it was in His goodness that God did.

In our lives, so often we want to find out the source of our affliction. We search to know whether we brought it on ourselves or if it was brought on by someone or something from an outside source. The thing I have realized is this: so many things that have happened in my life have been as a result of my own sin; others came out of nowhere and were of nothing that I could have changed or done differently. Here is the freedom: because of Jesus and His grace, regardless of the source, they were all filtered through God's loving hands. If He allowed it, He promises to use it. They have all brought me to the same place—His arms, more of Him. And each of them is nailed firmly and eternally to the cross. *All.* Oh, friends, there is so much liberation in this. My prayer for each of you in this very moment is that if the Lord has chosen you to pick up this book, that He would use these pages to bring you to a place in your life where you could cease looking at the affliction and instead look to Him. I pray that, by the Holy Spirit's power, you would be able to rest in your trials and suffering, knowing that it is through His goodness that He chooses each and every second of your life; and that you could see that He desires to use it all to make you and those around you more like Him. And then, one day, "...they will see His face, and His name will be on their foreheads" (Revelation 22:4).

While I may have to wait until I reach heaven to see Him face-to-face, I don't want to wait until then to experience His glory. I want to see God leading me to the land of milk and honey now, sometimes through the places where I least expect to see God's goodness. He is so very good. These words are written from a sinful woman, saved by grace alone, who has lived life desperate to see Him in it all.

By His grace alone,
Morgan

CHAPTER 1

IN THE BEGINNING

To love at all is to be vulnerable. Love anything and your heart will be wrung and possibly broken. If you want to make sure of keeping it intact you must give it to no one, not even an animal. Wrap it carefully round with hobbies and little luxuries; avoid all entanglements. Lock it up safe in the casket or coffin of your selfishness. But in that casket, safe, dark, motionless, airless, it will change. It will not be broken; it will become unbreakable, impenetrable, irredeemable. To love is to be vulnerable.

—C. S. Lewis

I THINK IT WAS THE first time I made eye contact with either one of them. There was no beeping around me, no malfunctioning machines, and no chaos on the intensive care floor at the moment—only she and I. Her entire hand was the size of my thumbnail. I could have practically held all four pounds, twelve ounces of her in one of my own hands. Those eyes had been shut almost the entirety of her first couple of days on earth, but in this moment, they were wide open—big, brown, and the most beautiful thing I had ever seen. Our eyes connected, and we just stared at one another, both of us seeming to ponder how we knew the other. I had longed to see what she and her sister would look like for many months, and now I was staring her directly in the face. *I was terrified.* The unconditional, heart-stretching love I had for her was undeniable, and I had the stark realization right then and there that I was responsible for her well-being. This miracle, this gorgeous human being, was mine. How could God have possibly entrusted this baby, albeit *two*, to my husband and me? Beyond that, how were we to possibly protect her, to protect them, from all the brokenness and the hurt this world contained? What if she got injured? What if someone was mean to her? There was no way that I could save them from everything. I had barely even changed a diaper, much less learned to forge a hedge of protection around the two most valuable beings on the face of the planet. *Terrified.*

My husband. My God-fearing, manliest of all men, hunk of a husband. We met in college at a Special Olympics meeting, and the moment we locked eyes, I was pretty sure that if he wasn't "the one," I sure wanted him to be. There was an obvious attraction from the beginning, but we had a lot of growing up to do before we said our vows. He, too, would say there was "something different" early on, but it took a few years (almost five to be exact) before he decided to take the leap of faith and get down on one knee. I get it. Our relationship was messy. We are both two very strong-willed, stubborn individuals, and from the get-go, we could somehow always find something to argue about. We were crazy in love, however, and we saw the God in one another from day one. Hugh was at the end of his second year of medical school when we said, "I do," and our wedding and honeymoon was that of a dream. I could not believe God had allowed me to marry that same man I saw at that Special Olympics meeting. You see, as I stated before, our relationship was far from perfect. We had been through everything from small misunderstandings to large betrayals, but the beauty in it all was that God had not only given us the grace to continue on, He had also begun the process of redemption and healing in our marriage as well. Through many solid mentors in his life, Hugh was becoming the spiritual leader that I had always longed for, and I was attempting to learn the art of submission and the freedom that comes from a marriage that reflects Christ's relationship with the church. Sure getting married during residency with all the time constraints and financial difficulties that it entailed was not the easiest thing in the world, but for the most part, we lived a seemingly normal, blissful life. I was a social worker at a therapeutic school for families who were considered high risk, and I could not have loved a job more. We got a puppy, spent some weeks doing mission work in Bangladesh, and just enjoyed our community and one another. Life was good.

When it came time to decide where Hugh wanted to spend the next four years of residency, God made it clear through a string of events and a lot of prayer that we were to rank Birmingham, Alabama, UAB Children's Hospital, number one. As match day approached, we were both excited to see what the Lord had in store for our little family. Hugh, in fact, matched at UAB Children's Hospital, and we began the process of setting up shop in a new city. God graciously opened up the doors for the move to be almost seamless. We found a house quickly, I got a job at an amazing adoption agency (Lifeline), and we found a church that quickly became our home (Church of Brook Hills). Through our church, we were able to get connected to a small group in our neighborhood within the first couple of months. We were in awe of God and His provision in so many areas of our life, and looking back, I see this as His goodness in providing community that we would so desperately need later on.

While we loved our small group, we were a little turned off by the fact that, outside of one other couple, they all had children. I have heard the same sentiment that I am about to share with you from many of my friends, and so I will put it simply: kids are not on your radar until the moment that they are. For a woman, I believe that once the first glimmer of an addition to the family enters her mind, it becomes a thought that shows up more and more frequently. For us, I remember the conversation clearly. We had left our small group after a particularly kid-filled (crying, screaming, distracting) night, and I was thinking about how peaceful our home was. Hugh, on the other hand, had a different thought: "Maybe we should pray about God's timing for trying to have kids rather than thinking about our own timing," he nonchalantly blurted out. When God told woman that her husband would "rule over" her in Genesis (3:16), I believe that qualified our emotions as well. All it took was for my gorgeous, manliest of all men, hunk of a husband to suggest a new bundle of joy for me to step—no, jump—on board. Truthfully I think Hugh was just making a suggestion and I was running off of emotion. I'm not sure either of us put much thought into the whole thing, but a few weeks later, I had a sneaking suspicion that something I had never experienced before was taking over my body.

When a pregnancy test (or ten) came back positive, I tried to come up with a creative way to tell Hugh because I thought that's what a good wife would do—"tried" being the key word. I was so overwhelmed that when he walked in the door, my plan went out the window, and I just blurted out, "We're pregnant!" I think it took Hugh's jaw about three minutes to come up off the floor, and then, like every good doctor would do, he went straight to his white coat and found something entitled, "The Pregnancy Wheel," a contraption that determined the supposed date of conception. I was confused and continued to ramble on about me being shocked too, allowing him to process things however he needed to do so. After seeing all ten of the positive pregnancy tests, and determining that there was, in fact, a possibility that we had conceived a child that month, we took time to pray. We had several friends and family members that were longing for a child but unable to conceive at that time, and so it felt selfish and a little mean not to recognize this baby as a gift from God in His perfect timing, just like we had wanted. After asking others around us about doctor recommendations (remember that we had just moved to a new city), we made an appointment for a few weeks later. Without realizing it, pregnancy had become such a glamorous thing in my mind. I would develop a cute little baby bump, have a fantastic glow at all times, and eat ice cream every night while Hugh rubbed my slightly swollen, but still adorably cute, feet. I had no idea what I was getting into.

Fast forward a few weeks to our appointment. I was already feeling extremely nauseous, and even the thought of eating ice cream sent me to the bathroom. Saltines, ginger ale, and bagels with cream cheese had become my only friends, and I was having a hard time waking up in the morning to get to work. I had begun to think I was some kind of pregnancy wimp, and I'm not sure Hugh wasn't contemplating whether or not the whole thing was in my mind. After all, at this point, I could only be about eight-weeks pregnant. Wasn't that a little soon for all these symptoms to be in full force? As we sat in the waiting room, we prayed for our baby, and I felt a sense of control come back into my mind once again. I am a control freak. At that point, I made daily to-do lists, organized my grocery list according to where things were located in the store, and liked to have my week semiplanned out by Monday. It's a little obnoxious at times but sort of the way I'm wired. Ever since I began understanding what it meant to truly find freedom in surrendering to the Lord, it has been a constant back-and-forth battle between me thinking I was "giving God the reigns" and me then "taking the reins back." He continues to give me reminders, both big and small, that He has had the reigns from the beginning.

As we stepped into the ultrasound room, the kindhearted technician gave me some instructions and set up the screen. The next few minutes are still a blur to me. I heard her say, ever so sweetly, "Well, guys, there are two sacs!" I looked up at my gorgeous, manliest of all men, hunk of a husband for some clarification. My immediate thought was that she was implying she could already tell it was a boy (remember, my husband is the doctor, not me). I heard Hugh say, "Oh, yeah...I see them," and then he mouthed, "twins," to me. It gets even blurrier from there. I would love to tell you I gloriously listened to the two heartbeats and giddily began to plan for our now double blessings, but that is far from the truth. I began hysterically crying, so much so that the kindhearted technician left the room to "give us a moment." Hugh is one of the calmest, most patient men I have ever known, and he seemed to be unfazed by the whole thing. He asked me what was wrong. I told him I was scared, and when he asked what for, I simply replied, "The rest of our lives!"

Truly it went much deeper than that. Sure, Hugh is a twin, but the gene tends to only be carried in females, and it almost always skips a generation. Yes, I had already been pretty sick and crazy exhausted, but I just assumed this was par for the course. The thoughts were zooming through my head at a faster rate than my brain could pick up: *How are we going to afford this with Hugh being in residency? How can I carry twins, much less raise them? Isn't a twin pregnancy considered high risk?* The thoughts went on and on. The bottom line is this: In that moment, I realized at a deeper level than ever before that I have absolutely no control over "my" life. To those of you who don't struggle with control (do you people even exist?), this is probably a no-brainer. For me, this was pivotal. I realized that any pseudocontrol I thought I had over my life was just that—not real! He is in control whether we choose to recognize it or not, and He is going to bring to pass those things that He chooses. The sooner we begin to accept this, the more peace we will experience. I did not realize at the time that this was just the tip of the iceberg in Him making that clear to me.

CHAPTER 2

NOT IN CONTROL
AFTER ALL

"Thus says the Lord, your Redeemer, who formed you from the womb: I am the Lord, who made all things, who alone stretched out the heavens, who spread out the earth by myself..."

—ISAIAH 44:24

WE LEFT THE KINDHEARTED ULTRASOUND technician and went to see my actual doctor for the first time. *Nice to meet you; you're pregnant, and there are two of them* was not exactly how this control freak would have liked our first appointment to go, but as my sister so often reminds me, "It is what it is" and "It was what it was." We talked about a lot of things, from what I could or couldn't eat to how our appointments would be going from then on. A moment that could have been missed but I can't go without mentioning is when she asked us if we wanted the genetic testing that was offered for high-risk pregnancies. Hugh and I looked at each other, shook our heads no, and then told her, "No, thanks." After all, we would not do anything differently regardless of what it said, and anything that would have showed up on that would bring more stress to the pregnancy, not less. I am not sure if anything would have shown up on the testing regardless, but I will be honest: I did not give it a lot of thought because I was pretty sure nothing was "wrong" with our babies. Why would it be? There was no family history, and neither Hugh nor myself had walked through challenging enough situations at this point to understand the reality that hard things do not "skip generations" or play favorites.

We left that appointment and determined to tell our family and friends immediately. I even began a blog in order to document the whole thing and share the lessons God was teaching me throughout the pregnancy. While it seemed a little early to share so much, both Hugh and I agreed that we would offer that information with others if something were to go wrong (plus, I was so sick that it was going to be a pretty hard thing to hide). More honesty: I didn't really think anything would go wrong. We really never do until it does.

Hugh began memorizing Psalm 139 the week we left that appointment. I began doing all that I could to have the healthiest, longest pregnancy possible. I am so thankful that God in His wisdom gave me the desire to stay away from anything and everything that was even potentially harmful for a pregnant person to eat or do. While human nature always causes us to wonder, "What did I do?" or "What could I have done differently?" I have not had to go through much turmoil with that because of the fact that I truly tried to be the healthiest pregnant person possible. I followed all food, exercise, and environment suggestions almost to a T. While we knew it was always a possibility that we would have our babies prematurely, for some reason, I didn't really worry about that. I truly felt the Lord carrying me through the whole thing and knew our babies were in the palm of His hand. Amid a lot of sickness and fatigue, the girls continued to look great, and we had no reason to believe they would be anything but perfectly healthy, developing children. I went into false labor around thirty-three weeks, but they were able to stop the labor and just put me on strict bed rest. I remember people telling me to enjoy it and to get as much sleep as I could. To someone who is pregnant and doesn't have children, this is quite annoying. Of course now I understand, but at the time, you feel like you are too uncomfortable to sleep, and you think in your mind that your bladder's inability to stay empty for more than a couple hours at a time is preventing you from getting any real rest. I was also confused as to why parents always complained about being tired. I mean, I had been sleepy before. What was the big deal? I could function on quite little sleep and be just fine, so I thought. Ha!

When I was thirty-six weeks and five days pregnant, I went in for my weekly doctor's appointment. While the girls' movement still looked great, one of the twins had not grown for a couple of weeks, which made my doctor think that it was probably time to deliver. I was relieved on so many levels, and the next morning, April 24, 2013, Ally Ruth and Bailey Grace Cheek made their entrances. The girls were both breech and therefore needed to be born via C-section. It was a seamless delivery, and both girls came to the room with me at first. Due to one low blood sugar and one low temperature, they were taken to the neonatal intensive care unit for observation. There were no breathing or feeding issues, and the nurses continued to tell us they were the healthiest babies they had taken care of in the NICU in a long time. We were blissfully grateful that everything seemed to be OK. While it was challenging for me not to have the girls in our room during our stay there, I was all too aware that we had an easy situation in comparison to some. At the time, I remember praising God for His absolute protection and provision in our little family's life. I thought we were in the clear for anything unusual, and while I could not be more wrong, I remember being in disbelief at how perfect the whole thing had been thus far. After a five-night stay in the NICU, the girls came home, and we began what I fondly refer to as "the newborn trenches."

Lessons Learned

- What does God's Word say about control? (Psalm 32:9, 1; Corinthians 7:37; Romans 8:6–8)
- What areas of your life do you find yourself struggling with the desire to be in control rather than trusting that God is in control?
- What would it look like to let go of control in these specific areas? (Think both emotionally and practically.)

CHAPTER 3

THE NEWBORN TRENCHES

"If God tears up your beautiful game plan and leads you into a valley instead of onto a mountaintop, it is because He wants you to discover His plan, which is more beautiful than anything you or I could have dreamed up. The response of trust is, 'Thank You, Jesus,' even if it is said through clenched teeth."

—Brennan Manning

"The first forty years of parenthood are always the hardest."

—Unknown

I HAVE BEEN AN AVID journaler for as long as I can remember. ("Journaler" is a word no matter what my spell-checker wants to tell me. Red lines, I ignore you. Readers, just go with it). In fact, I have often looked back with both embarrassment and intrigue at some journals hidden under my bed from when I was in elementary school. Yes, you heard that right: a ten-year-old, keeping track of her deepest and most profound thoughts. It seems I have always found both therapy and joy in putting my thoughts on paper. When I first began knowing Jesus, I became fond of prayer journaling. This became the easiest way for me to have undistracted time in communication with the Lord. It was also a great way to look back on God's faithfulness in my life. Our brothers and sisters in the faith did the same thing throughout the Old and New Testament, constantly speaking of God's faithfulness to the Israelites in the wilderness in the midst of their sheer unfaithfulness and mistrust in Him. I say this to tell you that during those first few weeks home with the girls, it was all I could do to muster up reading a verse here or there or journaling a one-sentence prayer. I had the following sentence written in this exact format:

04/ /13 (I am pretty sure I had no idea whether it was day or night, much less what day it was): You are daily fleshing me out. Thank You, Lord.

Daily fleshing me out. This pretty much sums up those first couple months of motherhood. When I got married, I had no idea how selfish I was. I always warn people who are about to get married and are in "giddy, blissfully unaware" mode that they are about to see more of their own sin than they ever knew existed. Sounds like a bubble-buster, but it is meant to be a loving encouragement that whenever they begin to feel this, they are not alone. Motherhood is like this on steroids. It did not take me long to understand the whole no-sleep thing. Yes, I had gone a couple nights here and there without much sleep, but this took it to a whole new level. The thing is that you didn't see a light at the end of this sleep-deprived tunnel. There was no relief. Combine that with a heavy dose of post-partum hormones and the fact that I had no idea how to take care of one, much less two, fragile little human beings, and you get somewhat of a mess—a sweaty, spit-up, sticky, poopy, exhausted mess. No one tells you how challenging this season is going to be, but I realized that they don't because there's really no way to explain it until you are walking it. It is one of those lessons that can only be learned when lived. This is not a motherhood-centered book, so I will not spend a lot of time discussing the ins and outs of what goes on in those first few weeks. I will simply say that my entire life was centered around nursing, pumping, changing diapers, washing baby clothes, holding babies, and trying to figure out what the heck I was doing while attempting to shower once every few days. However, this fleshing out was doing so much good for my soul. Sometime in May, I wrote the following: "Jesus, here I am. Whipped, wiped out, in the pits, and all Yours. So thankful You are using these girls to bring me to my knees again and bring Your word alive again. Praise God!"

Back when I was single and in college, I thought that once I got married and God determined sex was then a holy thing, all sin and temptation would dissipate. I realize now how crazy this sounds, but it seemed like so much of the focus was physical purity at that time. I was less than aware of the fact that we must be cleansed from the inside out. The Pharisees and Jesus had a similar conversation, and Matthew 23:26 says it this way: "You blind Pharisee! First, clean the inside of the cup and the plate, that the outside of it may become clean also."

Ugh, I can't stand it when I see myself in the Bible as the Pharisee in the story. I would rather be the sinner who was allowed at the table that the Pharisees are sneering at than the Pharisee himself and for good reason. Jesus was constantly getting on to the Pharisees for their lack of heartfelt worship. They continued to be more concerned with the outside appearance, with what man thought of them, than what God said or thought. I hate this. I don't want to be this. But in so many different seasons of life or areas of my current life, I see it more than I would like to admit. Anytime we make the focus of the Gospel anything but Jesus, we have missed the point. Yes, physical purity is important, but it isn't what saves us. Furthermore, as the Scripture says, my sin does not begin from the outside; my sin begins directly at the heart. Sometimes I think we prefer to think that our actions are what make us sinful because we pridefully forget that we are guilt-ridden through and through. The truth is that no matter how clean I make the outside look, my heart will still be broken. Without the grace of Jesus Christ, I am tainted with death. Anyway, I digress.

Here I was, locked in the prison of my own home with all temptations of the outside world clearly out of my reach, and I saw my sin more than ever. Motherhood will do that to you. In a way, the nature of motherhood feels somewhat isolating. It can be lonely, and it is a true example of servanthood. No one sees the trillion diapers you are changing, the hours you are holding crying babies, and the days spent nursing the baby who seems to live in a constant growth spurt—no one but God Himself. The verses in Colossians exhort us that, "Whatever we do, work heartily, as for the Lord and not men" (3:23). Why? Because we know that it is the Lord who we are serving; the Lord who will reward us. What will He reward us with? Himself (verse 24). Motherhood caused me to truly determine if that was enough, if simply serving Him on a day-to-day basis without affirmation or a "thank you" from those helpless babes was enough. As I decided that maybe it didn't feel like enough, but I wanted it to be so, God did a wonderful thing in my heart: He began the slow process of helping me live not out of my emotions, but out of Him. This is one of the things I love most about my Savior. He cares more about our hearts and our authenticity than the things that can be seen. And we can come to Him and ask Him to give us the desire to desire things! He takes ninety-nine steps, only asking us to take the one toward Him, walking not in the flesh, but in the Spirit (Galatians 5:16). You see, it wasn't that I had not been spending time in the word and setting my heart on knowing God more and allowing Him to sanctify me. It's just that sometimes, when we are comfortable and there is not much challenging us to look outside of ourselves and our own desires, we unfortunately choose self no matter what our intentions might be. Being a wife had helped me to begin to focus on myself less, and being a mom was forcing me to do so even more. Hard? Yes. Life giving? Absolutely.

I took the hard parts of this new season of life and placed it directly in His hands. Lamentations 2:19 says, "Pour out your heart like water before the face of the Lord. Lift your hands toward Him for the life of your young children." This was originally intended for the Israelites, but this is what I was doing—pouring my heart out like water, on my knees, begging God to help me survive this new and challenging season and praying to Him on behalf of Ally and Bailey Grace. I was letting go and giving Him their precious little lives, determining that they were safer in His hands than in mine. I had no idea how much harder this prayer would become.

Lessons Learned

* Whether you are married or single, a parent or not, what relationships or circumstances in your life have made you most aware of your selfish tendencies?
* Do you agree with the author that the process of being "fleshed" out is good for your soul? Why or why not? If yes, how have you seen this true in your own life?
* Reread Matthew 23:26. In what areas of your life do you need to be reminded to be cleansed from the inside out? To put it bluntly, where are you acting more like a Pharisee than a sinner saved by grace?
* Do you believe—truly believe—Colossians 3:23–24? How would it transform the way you view your daily tasks, whether at work or in the home, if you grasped onto this truth more fully?

CHAPTER 4

A NEW KIND OF HARD

""Beloved, do not be surprised at the fiery trial when it comes upon you to test you, as thought something strange were happening to you. But rejoice insofar as you share in Christ's sufferings, that you may also rejoice and be glad when His glory is revealed."

—1 PETER 4:12-13

LOOKING BACK, IT'S FUNNY THAT I thought our situation was difficult those first couple of months. I am not undermining the life of someone who has typically developing twins or even someone who has one baby. The newborn trenches are hard no matter what your scenario, and things are always relative. This is something I am learning more and more. For every person who has something less challenging to walk through, there will be someone who has something harder. For me, though, it is nauseating and humorous all at once to look back at what my definition of hard was. This is another thing that makes me love our Savior. He went to the cross and took on all the sin of everyone who had ever lived and who ever will live. He was perfect, and He took on imperfection willingly. He was betrayed by those He was choosing to die for, and as they spit in His face, He cried out, "Father, forgive them, for they know not what they do" (Luke 23:34). He is the ultimate example of someone who could have chosen to make a big deal of His situation, and none of us would think it was dramatic. He could have played the comparison game and won each and every time. But He didn't. Why? Because He was God and because He saw the bigger picture. Furthermore, He chooses to ask us to cast all our cares on Him (1 Peter 5:7). He wants to take on our burdens (Psalm 55:22). He does not ask for us to have something bigger and better than our neighbor in order to help us. Far from it. His strength is limitless, and there is enough to go around. Whether your hardship is a broken nail or a broken marriage, He wants to carry it for you. It's the very nature of who He is. How thankful I am that He has patiently and lovingly listened to me through all seasons and not dismissed my cares as too small. How I want to be more this way. Friends, we must seek to be like Jesus in all things. We must desire to be professional lovers who are motivated by His compassion in all we think, say, and do. He wants to be the source of this for us. We must internalize the mercy He offers us so that we can, in turn, pass it on to others. May we never be people who are so wrapped up in our own stuff that we don't empathize with those around us. I digress again.

So there we were, two or so months in and feeling great that both we and the girls had survived. People always ask when we first knew that something was going on with the Ally and Bailey Grace, and this is such a hard question to answer, both literally and emotionally. The short answer is I don't really know. The long answer is that the cycle of grief is a funny thing, and both Hugh and I stayed in a bit of denial for a while. We are forever grateful for those who trusted our God and our parental intuitions enough to allow us to process it all in our own time and we are learning to let go of some bitterness that came from those who did not. Those of you who are parents know how much you want to be able to protect your children from anything and everything that is less than perfection, and at some point, we all realize it is impossible to shelter them from it all. For those of us who have children with medical or developmental issues, this comes quicker than it does for others. It is gut-wrenching and at times, almost too much to take. I will get back to this in a little bit. The bottom line is this: it became apparent to our doctors, to family members and friends, and to us that something was just not typical with our girls. As they developed, they just seemed to be behind their peers in many ways. Like any parent would, we so desperately wanted to believe that the girls were going to catch up soon. I remember some of my and Hugh's early conversations about these things, the main thing being continued head lag at the time. Let me take this moment to say that while it has been more than difficult to be the momma in this situation, I don't envy being Hugh in the circumstance one bit. Here he was, trying to ease the worries of a hormonal, anxious new mother, all the more having the medical background that he does. He knew that he was not supposed to be the physician of his children, and he has continued to do an incredible job of letting their physicians do their job while stepping back and being the girls' daddy. However, he could not completely dismiss the knowledge that he had, and I often wonder how many nights he lay awake thinking of all the "what ifs" that could be. True, I had Google, but he had seen these things face-to-face and knew the reality of them. I will always admire the way that Hugh handled it all—asking his colleagues and attendings what they would do in our situation, continuing to pray, but not pushing panic buttons and prayerfully discerning when we should address it all. There I was, with no knowledge of what was typical or atypical, but assuming everything would be "just fine" according to what I thought was fine. At the girls' four-month appointment, we went ahead and made an appointment with some specialists and started the girls in early intervention—out of precaution, we told ourselves. Very truthfully, I am not sure if we believed this or not. Ally and Bailey Grace were not very interactive at this time. They were not interested in toys; and spent most of their days content laying on a mat and staring above. They were extremely content babies; children who would give a big grin as they fell into blissful sleep. There were not specific things that we could put our finger on, other than the head lag and them both being very "floppy" babies; yet something felt off. Once the girls were evaluated, we were all in agreement that the girls had "hypotonia," a word that has since become a part of my daily vocabulary but was foreign at the time. Essentially hypotonia is low muscle tone. It is different than strength and has more to do with the muscles' foundation than how strong or weak a child is. In most cases, it is a symptom of something rather than a cause itself. Every now and then, it is considered benign and is something that a child will just grow out of with therapy and in time. After looking up many of the causes, I determined right then and there that we were in the benign category. We had to be. I could not bear it if something was wrong with our girls, but more on that later.

At some point, we all realize that God's vision for our family is different than our own. For those of us who have children with unique needs, this truth comes all too quickly and is piercing to the core. I will never forget the moment we were told it was time to make an appointment with the neurologist. At the time, I did not know fully what that even meant, but I knew that it was not a place I wanted to be. We got the call that the neurologist would be able to see us on November 14—my birthday. When we explained this was my birthday and asked if there was another day, she told us that the next appointment would be in June. We told them we would bring cake and party hats.

I don't remember a lot about the time period between when we scheduled the appointment to when we saw the doctor, but I do remember looking up many possibilities of what "it" could be, realizing that there was a very good chance that it was something life threatening. While I knew that there was a possibility our life was going to look differently than planned, this was the first time I thought about the fact that it could be something that would take our girls from us. If you have been in this position, or even more, have actually lost a child, you will understand when I say that swallowing this truth was something I found impossible to do, but wanted to try in order to be as prepared as possible. I researched life-threatening reasons for hypotonia and watched video after video of children who had been diagnosed with one of these and since passed away. As morbid as this sounds, this was my way of trying to reach back for some control, and I recognize it as that. It was as if I was saying, "OK, here's the deal. I was totally unprepared for our reality, but if I can be prepared for any and all outcomes that are ahead, it won't hurt as badly because I will have somewhat seen it coming." I know this isn't true. But when you think you are waiting on finding out if the Lord is going to take your only two children, you do what you can to cope, and this was one of the things I reached for in attempts to process our new reality. In my better moments, I would spend time in prayer and cry out to God with worship songs that expressed my desire to continue to praise Him in the midst of the unknown and potentially unfathomable. God was doing an incredible work in my heart. He was teaching me to do the thing that, without Him, would be impossible. Sure there were moments where I would be taking care of the girls, have a moment where I saw them in all their helplessness and cuteness, and have to leave the room to shed the tears that wouldn't stop coming. But even then, He met me where I was and gave me the strength to carry on and to be the best mom I knew how to be. By the time we had reached the week of the appointment, I can honestly say that I was ready to say, as Job once had, "The Lord gives and the Lord takes away, blessed be the name of the Lord" (Job 1:21). This is nothing short of His sheer grace in my life. Coming from someone who, try as I might, lives by passion and emotion more than I would like to admit, to be taught to do otherwise is nothing short of supernatural.

On November 14, we tried to all act like everything was normal, and friends and family did a good job of remembering that it was my birthday on top of a very big appointment. Neurology appointments are nothing short of bizarre, and after talking about everything from what other family members looked like to the girl's sleep patterns, the doctor doing an examination, and then ordering a couple blood tests, the neurologist determined she wanted us to continue physical therapy but that we were going to "wait and see" how things went in the next few months. This became a common theme in our lives, this "wait-and-see" game. She said that if the girls were not sitting by the time they were nine months old (ten, adjusted for them), we would come back for further testing. We breathed a sigh of relief. You see, they were beginning to show signs of wanting to sit, and with their ten-month birthday being over three months away, I just knew they would be sitting by then. I couldn't believe that we had been given such good news. *Maybe that's it*, I thought. Maybe God wanted me to be able to let go of the girls and trust. Maybe the lesson is over.

Lessons Learned

* Think about whatever stage of life you are currently in. Where do you see God's vision for your family looking different than your vision?
* Think of a season of your life in which God's vision looked differently than you anticipated, yet He taught you to rejoice in His plans. If you cannot think of a time, why do you think this is so?

CHAPTER 5

MORE THAN I COULD BEAR

"Praise be to the Lord, to God our Savior, who daily bears our burdens."

—PSALM 68:19, NIV

"We are not called to be burden-bearers, but cross-bearers and
light bearers. We must cast our burdens on the Lord."

—CORRIE TEN BOOM

BACK TO THIS WHOLE "MORE than I could bear" stuff from the previous chapter. There were moments in this whole time period that I truly wondered if I could survive not only the waiting, but also the outcome. It got to the point where I was up at night, wondering what the next day would hold, and truthfully, I don't think anyone blamed me for it. God was continuing to teach me that my hope was in Him alone and that His word was the only thing that could truly be the balm for my aching heart, full of disappointments and fears. I clung to verses such as Psalm 94:19 that so eloquently reminded me, "When my anxious thoughts multiply within me, Your consolations delight my soul."

It was around this time that I felt the Lord calling me to blog again. I had not written since those early newborn days and was somewhat in a pattern of avoidance in general—avoiding questions about the girls, avoiding interaction with other typically developing children, just avoiding. As the new year tends to do, I determined to change this and gave in to the Lord's desire for me to share our story. On January 1, 2014, this is what I wrote:

No Such Thing as Mystery

Truth exists, and then there are lies. There is expectation, and then there is reality. There is the picture in our heads, and then there is the real story. And in the midst of those, God stands firm between the lines. He leads before and behind (Psalm 139:5). I have spent months praying and contemplating whether or not to share this portion of our family's journey. It feels more like Ally Ruth and Bailey Grace's story than mine. The Lord has clearly directed me to remember this however: it is *not* their story; it is *his* story. Hugh and I want to teach them that every moment of each of their lives. Any fears I have in sharing this season with you are directly trumped by the glory I *know* He is receiving. Therein lies our joy. God is working for our good. For Ally and Bailey Grace's good. And ultimately, He is bringing out more than we could possibly plan or imagine for the praise of Him and His kingdom. So here we stand.

Throughout my pregnancy, my prayer continued to be two things: that our babies would know the Lord in a real way at a young age, and that He would keep them healthy. Hugh memorized Psalm 139 during those months, and looking back on it, I see the Lord preparing us for where we are now. I was under the assumption that as long as we made it close to full term and there were no complications at birth, we were "in the clear" for any kind of health problems. The girls' fetal movement remained strong and consistent throughout my pregnancy. Although I went into labor at thirty-three weeks, they were able to stop the contractions and

I continued to carry the babies until almost thirty-seven weeks. The delivery was seamless, and while the girls went to the NICU for a few days out of precaution, nothing led anyone to believe we were bringing home anything other than two typically developing girls.

The months after we brought the girls home remain a blur. Between nourishing two babies, making sure they continued to gain weight, and basically just trying to make sure that they (and we!) survived, Hugh and I were busy to say the least. Slowly, the fog was lifted and we began to get used to our new normal. As time passed, it became obvious that there was some delay in the girls' development. I will spare the Internet many of the details, but the crux of everything is this: there was a point that I was convinced the Lord was going to take our two babies home. I say this with utter respect for those of you who have lost a child. I do not mean that in a dramatic way at all. But the words, "You give and take away" became very clear to me for a few weeks. Many doctors' appointments later, there are still no clear-cut answers. Some things have been ruled out, but we still lie in the gray. The one thing that has been determined is that the girls have hypotonia. What has not been determined, however, is what that will mean for them down the road. In the midst of doctor's appointments, physical therapy, and early intervention, we wait. For time to pass. For progress, or lack of thereof, to make its course. But at the end of the day, we are not waiting on any of these temporary things. We are waiting on the Lord. We are waiting on the God who is *the* Answer to *every* mystery. He is *never* surprised. He is not surprised by your story or mine because *he is writing it.* There are so many things that I want to relay to those of you who are reading this, but my ultimate purpose in sharing this journey is because I am firmly set in the truth that He is intricately sewing together the details of all our lives...and *all* the details are good. Whether we would have been told that the girls have a life-threatening disease or whether this turns out to be a "simple" developmental delay that is healed in time, He continues to be good and perfect in our midst.

There has never been a season of life that God has transformed my heart (or marriage) more. I cannot express how supported Hugh and I feel by the body of Christ. How our community has continued to encourage us. I cannot tell you that there has not been suffering. Comparison is the stealer of joy, and we have had to fight to remember that, just as Hugh memorized months ago, our girls are *fearfully and wonderfully made*. There is so much beauty in being able to celebrate and appreciate every milestone met, no matter how delayed. What I also want to portray and reveal to a watching world is that we rejoice in our sufferings because God never said that there would not be tribulations on this earth. The Lord sent His only Son to *suffer*. I have often found comfort in this truth: Jesus's purpose on this earth was solely that. To suffer for our sins. He counted it as a privilege because He was able to see the big picture. The glory in the aftermath. And while our humanity and flesh limits us from doing that, we can trust in the One who not only see it, but who painted it. We Christians have too often made it seem like if you follow Jesus, you will be "blessed" according to the worlds' standards. This couldn't be further from the truth. The Word of God does not define blessing as the world does. But there is *blessing in our suffering* because the *more we suffer, the more like christ we become.*

So, here we stand. In the gray. Without answers. With anxieties, sadness, disappointment, and fears. But more importantly, with our unchanging and sovereign God. This is His story. And so is yours. We can escape the bitterness and callous heart that comes from hard things when we look to Him as the Giver of ALL good gifts. If He has given it to you…it is good. This might sting today. It may not make sense today. Rest assured, the Lord grieves with us in our sorrows as well. But He allows circumstances and portions of our story to enter because He sees the beauty around the bend. While, of course, we are praying that God would heal the girls of any delay or atypical development that is occurring, we are ready to praise Him and trust Him if He, in His wisdom, chooses not to. And this, my friends, is where freedom lies. There is eternal beauty from all our ashes. Oh, how He loves us.

And there it was. Our life on display for all the world to see. Initially I wasn't even sure if anyone would read it. I just knew that I was supposed to share out of obedience. I could not have been prepared for the response I received—message after message of people thanking me for sharing our story, offering prayers for our girls, and encouraging me to continue writing. Just like that, God began using our girl's story as a platform for His glory. As I typed the words on the screen, a funny thing happened: I realized that the burdens were not only His to bear, but that He could handle them. All of them. Friends, do you have a worst-case scenario? Do you have a fear that you are positive would crush you if it became a reality? I am here to tell you that it wouldn't. You see, this first blog was just the beginning of the lessons that God was teaching us, and even looking back on it now, I see how far He has stretched me since. At the time, I thought that a couple simple blood tests put us in the clear for life-threatening diseases. It didn't but now, that's OK. He has walked me through enough that I am confident no matter what is ahead, He has written it all out. True, I said this in my blog. But as time has gone on, He has solidified this truth more and more. This is as real in your life as it is in mine. Whatever He has put in front of you, He is not going to leave you stranded in it as you cry out to Him. There is no fear, no worst-case scenario, that He hasn't already conquered at the cross. We are walking through what has been our hardest of hards, and He has continued to show us that there is no hard that He is not above. There is no circumstance, outcome, or situation that He cannot triumph. If He has put it there, rest assured that He is going to use it and that His strength knows no limit. Therein lies true freedom. We don't have to rely on the things of this world to escape the struggles of this life. In fact, we do not have to escape at all because if He has allowed it there; He promises to either bring us up out of it or walk us through it.

The next couple months were full of therapy, hard work at home, and more therapy. We were determined to get the girls to sit before their ten-month birthday. As I was sitting at home one afternoon, patiently trying to prop Bailey Grace up and watching her struggle to do so, tears stung my eyes. *Why is this so hard?* I thought. I put the girls down for a nap, and this time, I asked the Lord, "Lord, why is this so hard? We are all trying so hard. Why can't they just sit?" The Lord has never given me an audible answer to the questions of my heart, but in some moments, I hear Him speak ever so gently to my heart. This time was no different. I listened to Him as He spoke this truth, "Because maybe that's not what I want them to do right now. Maybe it's time to stop trying and time to start trusting." Ouch. Sometimes the truth just plain hurts, but it's what I needed to hear. I had been working so diligently to make the girls do what I wanted them to do without ever thinking that maybe it wasn't God's plans for them. I knew more letting go was going to have to ensue. I was going to have to let go of what I thought the girls' development should look like, and instead trust God with His perfect desires for them. *OK, I thought. They are Yours, Father. Do with them as You choose.*

Lessons Learned

* Where or when do you find yourself avoiding others or avoiding God? Why?
* Do you believe God is writing every detail of your story? Whether that answer is yes or no, which detail is hardest for you to believe is His good writing?
* Think of the specific season of life God has you in: What would be your worst-case scenario? Why is this so? Do you believe God could bring good from it if He chose to make that your reality?
* If you agree with the author that suffering can be a blessing, why is this so? Where has this been true in your life?

CHAPTER 6

BEYOND HARD

"Can you understand the secrets of God? His limits are higher than the heavens; you cannot reach them! They are deeper than the grave; you cannot understand them! His limits are longer than the earth and wider than the sea."

—JOB 11:7–9, NCV

"Our valleys may be filled with foes and tears, but we can lift our eyes to the hills to see God and the angels."

—BILLY GRAHAM

THE GIRLS WERE NOT SITTING on the day they turned ten months. In a way, the days prior began to prepare me for this, as I saw that their gross motor skills did not seem to progress. Hugh had already begun discussing next steps with our neurologist, and she was able to fit us in that upcoming Friday. I was so grateful for this; and my heart was already being made ready for this appointment. I wrote the following in my journal two days before we saw the neurologist:

Father,

I come to You in a place of rest. Resting in You. Resting in Your plan. Resting in Your goodness. The road ahead is unknown but I trust a knowing God…a good God. I am hurting. My stomach is in knots and anxiety about the "what-if's" and the future tear at my heart but You promise they cannot reach my soul and I praise You for that. I praise You for peace beyond understanding. God, I beg You to heal Ally Ruth and Bailey Grace. Beg You. I beg You to make no developmental delays, diseases, or diagnoses present in their lives. Heal them, Father. I know You can. I also know You are sovereign and Your ways are not mine. So, we trust You regardless. I pray that they would know You. God, I know they are already making an impact on Your kingdom. I praise You for that and pray it continues in Your sovereign goodness. Lord, You know the cries of my heart. The aching and gut-wrenching sorrow I feel when I think about them suffering at all. If I had the power to trade with them, You know I would. But, I don't have that power. You, however, did. And You traded with me at the cross. I thank You and praise You for that crazy amount of power. Father, I know in my heart You have healed them for eternity and I praise You already for that. Please don't leave me for even a second. Without You, I cannot do this…"

Tears flow down my face as I type this because it is still ever so real. The emotions are still present, and I continue to feel all these things. Something I want to make clear is this: God has not taken away the hard emotions we are facing. I still fiercely hurt over it all; I still want it to go away, but He has made Himself bigger, and He has caused me to fall so deeply in love with Him that all else fades in the distance when I think about His purposes and who He is. As David puts it in Psalm 73, "My flesh and my heart may fail, but God is the strength of my heart and my portion forever." The truth is this: our spouses, children, friends, jobs, hobbies, material things, and all else on this side of heaven are going to fade away.

They cannot offer us what we so desperately need for eternal significance. He, however, can. This is why I cling to Him instead of the things that are slowly, sometimes quickly, fading. Emotions can lie. Sometimes they are absolutely real in the moment, but they, too, are fading, and He still is bigger. We have to constantly give ourselves perspective in this through His Word and through the encouragement of those around us. So while, from the world's eyes, our girls should have absolutely been sitting by February 24, 2014, God's plan for them was different. During that season in particular, I found so much comfort in the story of Zechariah and Elizabeth from the book of Luke. They had prayed and prayed for a son. The world said that it was way past time for them to conceive and that it was wrong and even shameful that they could not. When they finally did become pregnant, while it was not in the world's timing, it was absolutely God's. He always has His intentions set on the bigger picture and not the smaller piece of the puzzle. Our specific seasons or timetables may not get answered the way we would choose, but we must trust Him to the core. So, like Zechariah and Elizabeth, we had to make the choice to trust God with Ally and Bailey Grace. They were made perfectly in His image. They were developing exactly as He planned before the beginning of time. And, although we had an expectation that appeared to have not been met, He was not surprised and was continuing to do things in His own timing. Let's take a time-out, dear reader, and focus on you. What is it for you? What is the deadline you have set that you just cannot seem to meet? The unspoken due date of a season set in your mind? The milestone or the expectation that *has* to be met whenever your family, friends, coworkers, strangers, society, or you says so? Friend, God has not held out on you. He has not made a mistake; He never has and never will. If you are in the midst of a "should" or "supposed to," rest assured that His grace and provision have triumphed over all. You may be shocked or disappointed, but He is not. He did this, in fact. In Christ, we are promised that every disappointment, unmet expectation, or atypical circumstance in our lives has already been met through Him who loves us and died for us before this world's rulebook ever came into play. And let me remind you that He has not forgotten you. He is not holding out on you. He is working all things together for the good of those that love Him. Yes, all things. Even that. He is working. He is sovereignly responsible in all things. He is good and will never forsake you. Thanks be to God!

The appointment on February 28, 2014 could be described in one word: hard. When we got to the office, I could already tell that the atmosphere felt different. Our neurologist walked in, and after examining the girls briefly, she said some words I will never forget: "I'm going to shoot you straight. I am very worried about your girls. I have a top-ten worry list for my patients, and your girls are number eleven and twelve. This is not benign hypotonia." She looked Hugh dead in the eyes as she said this, and then Hugh did something that he had not done since we had been married. He cried. Tears flowed down his cheeks, so much so that the neurologist offered tissues and the room became silent. I did not know how to react, but felt some sense of relief. It was as if I had been waiting for Hugh, the physician of the family, to admit the hard truth that this was not going to go away. This reality was both relieving and surreal. Suddenly I became as stoic as I had ever been. The grace of God has made Hugh and me somewhat of a seesaw in the sense that when one is down, the other tries to be up. While I couldn't exactly be up, I could at least muster out a neutral. I didn't know what to do with my gorgeous, manliest of all men, hunk of a husband crying. So I did nothing and tried to listen to her as she talked to us about what testing would be done next. I looked over at my daughters in the midst of all this, smiling and unaffected. I have continued to be a strong believer in the fact that they are listening to every word we are saying, and as she went on and on about the many conditions the girls might have, I could not imagine being them. Suddenly it became less about Hugh and me and more about the girls who were going to have to live with whatever this was for the rest of their lives. It didn't seem fair. I knew that other people were being positively impacted through their story, but what about them? Why did they have to walk through this so the rest of us could depend on the Lord more? I will go back to this later.

We did some more blood work, scheduled an appointment with a geneticist, made a date for an MRI to be done, and left with heavy, heavy hearts. The roller coaster of our life was beginning once again, and I was ready to get off and step onto a safer, more predictable ride. But God.

Lessons Learned

* Do believe that you can rest in God and experience hard emotions simultaneously? Give an example from your life (or the life of a friend or family member).
* Where have you seen God's timetable looking different than your own? How has God used that for His good in your life and the life of those around you? If in a group, this would be a good time to encourage one another in how others in the group have done this for you.
* Think of the hardest circumstance your family has walked through. Share with the group how God's grace helped your family to rely on His strength and the comfort of community during this time.

CHAPTER 7

MORE THAN WE COULD ASK FOR OR IMAGINE

"Now to Him who is able to do far more abundantly than all we ask or think, according to the power that works within us, to Him be the glory in the church and in Jesus Christ throughout all generations, forever and ever. Amen."

—EPHESIANS 3:20

"It would seem that our Lord finds our desires not too strong, but too weak. We are half-hearted creatures, fooling about with drink and sex and ambition when infinite joy is offered us, like an ignorant child who wants to go on making mud pies in a slum because he cannot imagine what is meant by the offer of a holiday at sea. We are far too easily pleased."

—C. S. LEWIS

AFTER WHAT CAN BE COINED as the "hard" appointment, we tried to get used to our new normal, even though we didn't really know what that meant. We saw the geneticist who sent off a panel of many tests, which he let us know would not come back for two to three months. The girls had an MRI, both of them came back clear, and we began the waiting game while trying to process that our life was most likely going to look differently than most people we knew. The things that kept me up at night at this point were not the "whys"; I thought a lot about future logistics. What areas of the girls' development would be permanently affected? Would they ever be mobile, and if not, was there a van big enough to fit two wheelchairs? Could I even push two wheelchairs? All of our physicians had been intrigued with the fact that the twins both had what seemed to be an autosomal recessive disease. This part actually continues to make me smile. I know that many people probably think it's more challenging that it is both of them. For me, it is a clear reminder that God is up to something. There is simply a very small chance that they would both have "this," whatever "this" is. Obviously God's plans trump all things. Medically bizarre? Yes. God ordained? Absolutely. When we went to the genetics appointment, however, he seemed pretty confident that while he didn't know what was going on, it certainly had to be genetic in order for two children to both carry it.

There has always been some tension that exists whenever Hugh and I discuss what is going on with our girls as genetic. Everyone seemed to be fine with talking about us going to the neurologist, but once it was suggested that we should see a geneticist, people almost got defensive for us. "Surely it's not genetic," they would say. It is as if people wanted to rationalize alongside us that this all happened at random, and that it could not happen again, almost as if it is separate from Hugh and myself. The thing is that no matter how much we would like to think that, it isn't. In a sense, openly taking about the girls having a genetic disorder felt as if Hugh and I were admitting something within us was defective. This is obviously not saying that we think our girls are anything less than perfectly created and formed. We love them exactly how they are, without doubts, and are so proud of them for no reason other than that they are ours. They being said, if we are being honest here, we all know Hugh and I would have chosen a more "normal" for them if we had been given the choice. Let's talk about this "normal" stuff. As I said earlier, I struggle a lot with the fact that it seems like Ally and Bailey Grace got the short end of the stick here. We all grow in our faith and see God through them, and they just suffer through their mediocre lives. Right? Wrong. Even as I type that, I know it to not be true. Bailey Grace and Ally are two of the most content little girls I have ever been around. They genuinely love their lives. Most days, they wake up singing, go to bed smiling, and exude joy like no other. They are truly happy. We are the ones who are discontent for them, and I believe this is because we assume we have an idea of what their normal should be. We all do this. We determine what we think people's lives should look like, and if it is different, we think it is less than perfect. How arrogant and how opposite of what the Lord teaches us. God promises us that He has plans to prosper and not harm us (Jeremiah 29:11). He promises us that because He gave us His own Son, He will offer us all things (Romans 8:32). That being said, any ideas of what we believe should be different about the plans for Ally and Bailey Grace are just that—ideas. They are not truths, and they are certainly not better than the things God has planned for us. I do not know the details of their lives; I do not know how numbered their days are, but this I do know: it is God's best. It is His perfect plan for them, and when they get to heaven, the crowns He puts on their heads will be full. Not only that, but their bodies will no longer be wasting away. If that phrase offends you, let me remind you that we are all dust. All of our physical bodies are fading, and all of us are dying. This is true for both Christian and non-Christian alike. Christians, however, have this promise:

> So we do not lose heart. Though our outer self is wasting away, our inner self is being renewed day by day. For this light momentary affliction is preparing for us an eternal weight of glory beyond all comparison, as we look not to the things that are seen but to the things that are unseen. For the things that are seen are transient, but the things that are unseen are eternal (2 Corinthians 4:16–18).

How much more do our physical inabilities and struggles point us to this crucial truth? Joni Eareckson Tada said once that her paralysis has drawn

On milk and honey

her closer to God and given her a spiritual healing, which she wouldn't trade for a hundred active years on her feet. We have prayed for our girls since we knew of their existence that they would know the Lord in a real way at a young age. Isn't this an answered prayer? Friends, things are not always as they seem. We are to fix our eyes on the unseen because those are the things of eternity. For us, just because what the Lord has for our girls on this earth appears to be less than ideal, that does not mean that it is not exactly what they need. What about you? What has He chosen to place in your life that you doubt is His best? What He allows in your life, He may not allow in mine. Don't miss this part: if He allows it, He promises it is good (Psalm 84:11). If He allows it, rest assured that it is a vital part of this journey you are on and a lesson that you could not have learned any other way. Our God is not only creative, He is perfectly intentional. He is not up in heaven throwing random bombs down on people without any purpose as to where they land. That is chaos, and we are promised that He is *not* the author of confusion (1 Corinthians 14:33). No, friend. He is absolutely in control, and rest assured that if He makes a choice for your life, it is essential for your growth and in His plans for you. This is why we do not have to believe the lie that creeps in that tells us we should wish for what our neighbor has or that we or those we love are in fact getting the short end of the stick. God choosing something for someone else has nothing to do with that which He has chosen for you. Whatever He has put in your life is His absolute best for you. Believe it! Believe it in the good times and bad, in the hard things and seemingly easy. After all, think about Christ, who was a sinless God-man walking on this earth, watching others around Him sin knowing that He was about to carry the weight of it all, knowing He was about to die a horrendous death for that which He did not do. He and the Father were one, and He knew that the journey He was about to walk had to happen. Why? Because it was God's best. He now sits at the right hand of the Father because of it all. Whatever is in your life today, it is good. It is nothing short of exactly what you need. Whatever is going on with our girls is God's best for them; He is not cheating them of anything. While their normal may look different than we anticipated, all of their days are perfectly ordained and planned out. Not one of them has slipped through His good and loving hands.

Back to genetics. In the beginning, I had to fight thoughts that continued to sneak in. This "something wrong" that they keep speaking of... this was a direct product of the love Hugh and I have for each other. How? And why? You see, I could get all bent out of shape when physicians said the phrase, "something wrong," but if I stepped of my politically correct horse for a minute, I knew what they mean when they said it. While our girls are made in God's image and intricately formed exactly how He intended, there was something wrong. There are literally pieces of me in my girls, and some of the frustration I felt in it all had a lot to do with the fact that it caused me to face my own disabilities, my own wasting away, each and every day. But here's the thing: there is something gravely wrong in all of us.

We pass a lot of things on to our children and pick up a lot of things from our parents. You don't have to look at a strand of DNA to see pieces of yourself in your children or pieces of your parents in yourself. Some of them are seemingly good, and some of them are not so good. Many of them are just plain awful. You see, the most dangerous genes we pass on to our children have nothing to do with physical ability, disease, or development. We have all passed sin on to our children, and there is nothing we can do about it. It is a part of our fleshly makeup. You don't have to go to a genetics appointment to see that played out in lives all around us, including our own. Generation after generation of sin pours out and injures the lives of those we love and those all around us. If Hugh and I were to have another child, even if we didn't pass on the same disease, we would ultimately pass something on to them that we wish we could erase. As Paul says in Romans, the things we want to do we do not do, and the things we don't want to do we do. Sometimes the reflection of us in our children's lives is just painful. We see our own brokenness and mistakes, and we cringe because we know it is a part of us and feel responsible in some way. Sometimes it is a lesson we have already learned, and we so wish that they would choose to not learn the hard way like we had.

From another view, many of you have had broken relationships with one or both of your parents, and the thought of seeing any tiny part of them in you makes you sick. If you are honest, you do see parts of them there, and you hate it. You would do anything you could to change it. For others, you never knew your biological parents, and it remains a mystery "why you are the way you are." It all seems so broken, doesn't it? We *all* seem so mutated and defective when we look at it this way. And we are. But Jesus.

Before Christ came, Jewish people were asked to take care of each sin in a particular way, even the sins they did not know they had committed. They would bring sacrifices to God as a payment for their sins, a payment for the broken parts of them that did not meet up to God's perfect standard. Before Christ came, Jewish people were the only ones considered God's chosen people. It was *all* about genetics. But Jesus.

God promises us that He came not to heal the healthy, but the sick (Matthew 9:12). He is the Great Physician, and He came to heal that which was most broken, namely our souls, through the medicine of His blood on the cross. We are sick, but He took our illnesses and bore all our diseases (Matthew 8:17). Christ became a curse for us. In Him, all our frailty and humanity was nailed to the cross (Galatians 3:13). Yes, even that. Even that thing you saw in your mother and swore you would never do but find yourself drowning in. Even that fear you have that one day, you, too, will be burdened by the mental illness that has stricken so many in your family—the tendency toward anger, control, bitterness, or defeat or the propensity for whatever kind of cancer or disorder. No matter what happens on this side of heaven, He nailed that to the cross. Yes, even that. While all hell seems to rage within us or around us, He promises that if we are in Him, if we have accepted in faith what He did for us on the cross, we are a new creation for all eternity. What's more, this offer is no longer just for those whose DNA matches up as God's chosen; this offer is for all who would yet believe and accept it as truth (Galatians 3:29; Ephesians 3:6).

If Hugh and I lived in BC times, we would have had to make sacrifices day after day for Bailey Grace and Ally Ruth because of the cultural belief that their unique needs were bad or wrong. But Jesus. In John 9, Jesus absolutely smashes this false thinking into the ground whenever a blind man is brought to Him. His disciples ask Jesus who did the wrong in that particular situation, the man or his parents. Jesus responds by saying, "It was not that this man sinned, or his parents, but that the works of God might be displayed in Him."

Aha! Because of Christ, none of our genes are relevant anymore. The only thing that is relevant is God and His glory. Anything in us, the things we would have chosen and the things we could have done without, can be used for His glory and our good. Generational addictions? He died for that. Gluttonous tendencies? Nailed to the cross. Social anxieties, infertility, physical and mental disability...the list goes on and on. I am not saying that these things do not exist on this side of heaven. They do. We live in a broken world, and pain and suffering are present everywhere we go. But it is for freedom that Christ set us free, and that freedom comes from knowing that one day He is going to redeem these bodies just like He has already redeemed our souls. You are a child without blemish in Christ (Philippians 2:15). Total healing will not occur until the day we meet our Maker, but He is sanctifying us day by day. Even if you cannot see it, if you are in Christ, trust that He is making you more like Himself as you look to Him to do so.

The girls future felt so unknown; and I had to fight to trust that His plans for them were good. It's OK if you are there too. Remember all that stuff about feelings we have been talking about? They are fleeting. We may feel broken, but I am encouraged that when Jesus came to earth, He was made like us in every respect except sin. He felt the things we felt, and He is walking through all our moments with us. He truly and fully understands your "now," whatever it may be. He has overcome the depravity of this world already, and there will be a moment in which we will see Him face-to-face and all else will fade. One day, we will look at Him in all His glory and know that it is, in fact, finished. He is the one who matters, and He has given His perfect genes to you, to me, and to Ally and Bailey Grace. Whatever He has in our today is working up a tomorrow that we could not have ever dreamed up. This caused me to find hope in the waiting and in the hard. He is so very good. It is easier to believe this when I see His active hands all around me; it was much more challenging, however, to trust this when all seemed to go silent.

Lessons Learned

- If you knew/know your biological parents, what qualities about them do you see in yourself that you like most? That you like least? If you have never met your biological parents, what do you most wish you knew about them?
- How does 2 Corinthians 4:16–18 make you feel about your so-called weaknesses? Do you see God using your weaknesses, whether physical or other, to bring Himself glory? If so, how?
- What are you most excited about God making new one day (see Revelations 21:5; Isaiah 43:18–19)? This can be in your own life or the life of a friend or family member.

CHAPTER 8

LAUGHING AT THE TIME TO COME

*"An excellent wife who can find? She is far more
precious than jewels…strength and dignity are her
clothing, and she laughs at the time to come."*

—PROVERBS 31:10, 25

LAUGHING AT THE TIME TO come. Totally not fazed by the elephant that was constantly in the room. How I longed to be this woman as we waited for more test results to come back. It seemed easier to trust in God when we had lots of appointments and discussion going on about the girls' development, but once things settled down and we began the waiting, I found myself even more perplexed. All around me, I felt like people were simply living life. Having babies, watching them grow up, commenting on "how fast it goes" without any idea of what their reality could be if God had chosen a different path for their family. I did not find bitterness in me; I knew that God was sovereign and in charge. I just found myself wanting answers and wishing the silence would go away. I wanted to be the wife and mom who was able to just "let go and trust" as far as diagnosis was concerned, but more often than not, I found myself consumed.

I prayed and hoped that by the time the girls turned one, we would have answers. It seemed realistic, but as their birthday got closer, I started thinking that maybe this wasn't going to happen. I have always been the person that thought it was crazy when people made their children's birthday parties elaborate. First off, they are young and will not remember it. Secondly, it is not exactly teaching them that the world does not revolve around them. With the girls' first birthday looming, I told numerous people that I wasn't going to make it "like a circus." However, with pending test results, I suddenly began to find reason to make it all the more special. After all, if we were being honest, we had no idea what the rest of their birthdays were going to look like, and we were not guaranteed that there would be another birthday. It got me thinking: none of us have the luxury. We have no idea if we will be here one second and gone the next. Shouldn't we always live in light of this? This new carpe-diem-like attitude is what led me to make their party less simple and more of one big celebration with all our family and friends. It also caused me to grasp onto the idea of "laughing at the time to come." When we trust the God, who knows each of our moments and is in control of our first and last breaths, we can simply laugh at any and all things because we know that whatever is to come is good. As a believer, what's the worst thing that could happen? We die and go to be with Him? Isn't that actually the best thing? Is that not what we are longing to do? I think sometimes that when life gets comfortable, we forget this. We take on an attitude that says, "I want to come live with you forever, Jesus, but I am not quite yet ready for that forever to start." The more we have been walking this journey with the girls, the more I see the brokenness and confusion of this world, and the more I long for heaven. Psalm 112:7 says, "He is not afraid of bad news; his heart is firm, trusting in the Lord. His heart is steady; he will not be afraid."

Not afraid of bad news. This was an attitude I wanted my heart to grasp. If I was living in light of eternity, holding on to the One who knows all our days, I could laugh in the face of all news, knowing it was all part of His glorious plan. I did not sense this every day, but during the months leading up to Bailey Grace and Ally's birthday, I truly felt God preaching this to my soul. I began to live in light of eternity and a greater plan rather than in the valley of my own grain of sand in the midst of the vast beaches of the earth. And, you know what? His word is true. It brought me authentic joy and peace that replaced my questioning and my wrestling. In light of knowing His promises, I was able to sing along with the angels, "You are worthy, our Lord and God, to receive glory and honor and power, for You created all things, and by Your will they were created and have their being" (Revelations 4:11).

He was worthy. He had always been worthy, but I was beginning to know this at a level that brought more freedom than words can express. In light of His worthiness, I could let Him be God, and I could just be me. I could plan the girls' first birthday party with or without a diagnosis, knowing that it was for freedom Christ set me free and that there was freedom in trusting Him with the things much greater than me. So I planned. There were definitely moments of sadness, thinking about what I pictured the girls' party to be like versus what it was going to be. Blasted expectations. We have them in so many different seasons of life, and most of the time, they are never met. This, too, was helping me to place my hope and my expectation in my God rather than what I thought things were supposed to look like. The truth is that these ideas in our head are just that—ideas. They are not reality, and He knows best and unfolds our lives with His perfect knowledge and wisdom. So all the thoughts I had about what should be (they cannot crawl at their party, they can't sit on a blanket with their "baby friends," they cannot eat birthday cake, etc.), I had to place these at the foot of the cross and allow Him to replace them with His peace. We decided that we would have an ice cream party, and we even had the girls try ice cream beforehand to make sure it was going to be a success. I just wanted them to feel loved and celebrated in the biggest way possible. I wanted to do everything I could to make them feel important and special. As I continued to plan, it got me excited about the party that will occur in heaven when we see Him face-to-face. All these years of us using faith as sight will be replaced with eyes to see. What a glorious day it will be! No tears, no hurts, no sickness, and no more death. Forever whole! It also brought to my attention how much more He must love us. Matthew 7:11 says, "If you who are evil, know how to give good gifts to your children, how much more will your Father who is in heaven give good things to those who ask Him!"

Here I was, an imperfect human, desiring to give my children the best things possible. How much more would God want to do that for us?

The Bible says, "He would did not spare his own Son but gave Him up for us all, how will He not also with Him graciously give us all things?" (Romans 8:32).

In light of all this, I began to feel genuinely excited about His plans for our little family. I began to realize in a deeper way that whatever He was offering us was good. His very best was given to us, and that was something to celebrate both at their party and forever. We had gotten so caught up in diagnosis and development that I had forgotten our main purpose with Ally and Bailey Grace: to show them the love of God and to have them know that love deeply. He had given us a full year with these baby girls. It could have gone differently. Yes, things looked differently than I could ever have anticipated, but His plans were still good, and He always has more up His sleeve. Forget my silly expectations and my less-than-perfect plans. I was ready to celebrate not only the first year of life with Bailey Grace and Ally, but also whatever He had chosen as our future.

Lessons Learned for Chapter 8 will be included with the next chapter.

CHAPTER 9

HAPPY BIRTHDAY, DEAR PRECIOUS ONES

This is directly from the blog I wrote the day before the girls turned one.

I woke up with tears brimming in my eyes today. Tears of joy and gratitude for all that the next few days represent. This time last year, I was headed to what would be my last doctor's appointment before our lives were forever changed for the good by our baby girls. **For the good.** I was uncomfortable, sick, exhausted (or so I thought...I didn't quite understand what exhaustion was before I went through the newborn trenches), and mostly anxious for getting our baby girls here "happy and healthy" as we all say (That phrase now is one of my pet peeves, which will be addressed at a later time). We had been praying the Lord would bring us our girls in His perfect timing, not one day sooner or one day later. Hugh had memorized Psalm 139, which is more symbolic than I could have ever known, and we were a lot of things. We were mainly clueless. The beauty of parenthood. We all start out that way, so blissfully ignorant. We have never met our little ones, and we all prepare as best as we can for the journey to come. **Girls, on April 23, 2013, there was nothing that could have prepared daddy and I for the beauty and joy that was around the corner on**

April 24, 2013. There are more lessons that the Lord has taught us through your sweet lives than we could recount, many that are written on the pages of this blog. I will not be able to word or express all that I want to share with the world as we await your first birthday tomorrow, but I want to give it a try because **daddy and I are indebted to you and the lessons that we have learned through your little lives already**. In a sense, this is a letter to You, my God; my version of a Psalm of praise for giving us more than we could possibly ask for or imagine (Ephesians 3:20). When we first found out we were going to have twins, I reacted as gracefully as it comes; I cried profusely as the ultrasound tech attempted to find two heartbeats through my hysterics. She left the room to "give us a moment" (yes, it was awkward), and when Hugh asked me what I was crying for, I said, "I'm scared." He responded, "Of what?" I quickly sobbed back, "The rest of our lives." **Girls, momma is no longer scared**. While you have already brought more twists and turns than we could have ever anticipated, I have learned to celebrate each and every moment of each and every day because of you. I have seen that there is nothing to fear around the corner because God is already there. I never thought I could have survived a year with twins, much less a year with twins as special as you two. But you know what? God is good and He has already walked this road for us therefore with Him, I have been able to step forward with confidence that whatever comes next is for His glory and our good.

Ally Ruth and Bailey Grace, we are proud of who you are. Not only that, but we wouldn't want you to be any different. Your beauty radiates from the inside out. Ally Ruth: your smile is absolutely contagious. Bailey Grace: your easygoing attitude is something that the rest of us would be wise to follow suit on. You both simply make people happy by your mere presence. The best part about this is: **it isn't because of anything you have done or are doing; it's merely because of who you are as a whole**. I could write a novel on all the amazing qualities you possess, but I would be amiss because that's another lesson we have learned: **it is not about you. Or me. Or any of us. It is about Him.** You have reminded us that we can see Him in anything and everything, even our worst nightmares, if we just would choose to look. **We are so very proud of you both for no reason other than that you are who you are.**

There is so much to celebrate tomorrow, but the fact that you are here "happy and healthy" will not be one of them. Karni Liddell, a Paralympics athlete that happens to have Spinal Muscular Atrophy, has said, "What does that even mean?" We have all said it, myself included, but here is the truth: **we didn't just want you here "happy and healthy." We wanted you here so you could live the lives that God intended you to live, which would ultimately bring eternal joy that stems beyond any temporary happiness or pseudohealthiness.** And, however long He sees fit to keep all of us on this side of heave, we will all continue to try and live that out, albeit imperfectly. The thing is, you both already seem to be more comfortable in your own skin than most people I know...**and that's contagious.** You live life above the circumstances around you, and have taught us to do the same. Sure, we might have thought your first year of life would have included more milestones and less doctor's appointments; more careless living and less therapy appointments. But, **watching you both accept each day with all it entails with such an attitude of contentment and trust has taught your daddy and me to do the same and for that, we wouldn't change a second of it.** I could go on for days, but it is time to feed you guys and I want to breathe in these moments. Bottom line is this: If I could go back and do it ALL again—the constant morning sickness that never seemed to end, the sleepless nights, the unknowns, the worries, the testing, the sheer terror that came the moment I realized that my heart was sliced in two and came out in the form of two precious, beautiful baby girls—**I**

would do it again a hundred times. To call being your mommy a privilege would be an understatement. I know I don't deserve to be. All praise, glory, and honor to the One who gives us grace upon grace in this journey. **Lord, *thank you*.** Bailey Grace and Ally Ruth Cheek: we celebrate you today, tomorrow, and every day after that. Happy almost birthday, sweet girls!

I MEANT IT. I MEANT every last word of it to my very core. And as I typed those sentiments, I was taken back to that moment in the NICU where I locked eyes with Ally. Then, I was terrified. *Now, I was carried.* I started out those moments thinking that it was up to me to take care of the girls and to ensure they were all that they could be; God had taught me that He was holding each of us all along and that He was going to make sure they turned out exactly as He had planned. His purposes, not my own. The moments all His, never mine. I was no longer scared of the little or big things that might come our way. After all, I had already faced the moment in which I realized who I was and whose they were, and my white flag had gone up. He was God, and I was not. I was simply their momma; He was their Savior, Father, and One True Love. It was His choice as to when they would take their first breaths, and it would be His choice as to when they would breathe their last. This would be scary if I had not realized in an even deeper sense that He was so very good. In The Chronicles of Narnia, C. S. Lewis puts it this way:

Edmund: "Is he safe?"
Mr. Beaver: "Safe? Who said anything about safe? 'Course he isn't safe. But He's good. He's the king I tell you."

This is what we had walked that past year. Not a second of it had felt safe, but in all of it, He was making His goodness known to us. Because of this, I was able to walk forward, not with confidence in my emotions, the roller coaster of doctor's appointments, others' opinions, or my own thoughts; I was able to walk forward with confidence in the one true God who stays the same in all of our days and who has the foresight to know what is best in all of our moments. True security. A safe landing into eternity versus a comfortable gallop in the temporary. So, celebrate we did.

On the morning of the girls' birthday, Hugh went and got flowers for them. This warmed my heart immensely, mainly because it was something that I did not suggest in the least. It showed me that he, too, felt like that day was special. He had even taken the day off of work, and days off were far and few between. We sat the flowers, gifts, and cards on their high chairs and planned on going to get doughnuts that morning. Normally, I am a ninety-nine-cent card kind of woman, but today was different. The girls both have an affinity for music, and when I found Disney cards that both played music, I knew that I had to get them (even though the cards cost about as much as their presents themselves!) After opening cards and presents and talking to the girls about how loved they were that day and always, we went to a local doughnut shop. We were pretty sure the girls wouldn't even want a bite (we were correct!), but we wanted to spend the entire day having fun. The rest of the day consisted of going to the zoo, going on a stroller walk, and having lots of diaper and movie time. What one-year-old doesn't enjoy being naked and watching television?

Back to those blasted expectations. Something that hasn't been mentioned is that the girls do not eat table foods and have not showed much interest in them up to this point. I did not think that cake was going to work for their party, and I was pretty sad about it. Of course, in the bigger picture, cake is not a huge deal either way. For me, it was more about what it represented that was painful. It was yet another thing I had to place in God's hands. I had decided, though, that every kid needed a birthday cake and candles, whether he or she was going to eat it or not. I got them a huge icing-covered cake, and we decided to invite one of our best couple friends, the Mercers, over for dinner and dessert. Before the girls went to bed, we lit the candles and sang, "Happy Birthday!" We gave them each a little lick of icing, which they didn't love but didn't hate. I cried. As a momma who had hurt a lot the past year, God offering me that simple moment made me feel so very loved; and I think it did the same for our girls. After the girls went to bed, we had a steak dinner and all went around the table and said how God had used Bailey Grace and Ally to teach us all different things in their short lives. Naturally this was my idea, but our friends not only agreed to participate, but gave Grammy-worthy speeches as well. My heart was full, and there wasn't a dry eye at the table.

You know, I do not know how much of April 24, 2014 our girls comprehended. I know that no one-year-old will remember his or her first birthday, no matter how memorable. I do know that it was a day that goes down as one of my most favorite days I have ever experienced, and that as Ally and Bailey Grace's mother, I could not have been prouder and felt more privileged than to spend the rest of my days being their momma.

That next weekend, we had their birthday party that included family and friends. It was an ice-cream-sundae celebration, and almost fifty people showed up! The weather was perfect, and we could not believe how many people had made an effort to show up, especially our friends Sarah Jane and Chase, who drove from out of town, along with the rest of our immediate family. I had built this day up so much in my head, and my prayer had been that it would be a happy day, not one spent looking around at what could have been. God loved me so well that day and caused me to focus on what truly mattered: His glory in it all. Sure Ally may have been a little freaked out by the crowds and ended up napping instead. Yes, neither Bailey Grace nor Ally could crawl around in the grass or sit on a blanket with the other kids. But as I breathed in deeply the reality of all God had given us, I knew we were more than blessed. I felt His presence that day, and it was more than enough to satisfy me. God was making Himself known more in our girls' short lives than many could say after an ample lifetime on this earth, and I knew He was doing more behind the scenes than I could ever imagine. There was more waiting around the corner, but on that beautiful May Saturday afternoon, all I saw were the joys He had placed all around us. It truly was the best birthday ever.

Lessons Learned

* What do you think it means to "laugh at the time to come" (Proverbs 31:10, 25)? Does this come easily for you? Why or why not?
* What is something that, like the author had to do with the hope of a diagnosis before Ally and Bailey Grace turned one, you have had to "lay at the foot of the cross"?
* The author says, "Back then I was terrified...now, I was carried." Can you relate? If so, how?

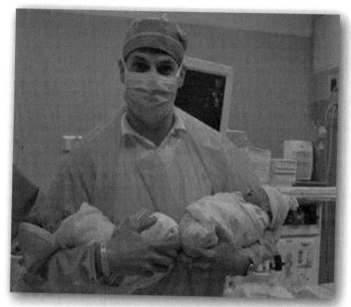

A proud daddy and his girls, April 24, 2013

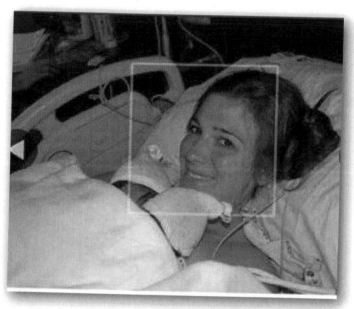

Welcome to the world, A and BG!

Holding hands from the beginning

Joy exuding at all times, Ally (left) and Bailey Grace (right)

Enjoying the Lakeshore Foundation pool with
daddy, one of our favorite pasttimes

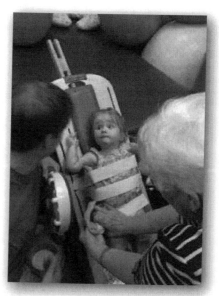

Ally, getting up in the stander for the first time at one of our
many physical therapy appointments with Patrice

Family pictures with Stacy Richardson photography, May 2014

Bailey Grace having a blast at her 1st birthday party with her KK and Big Ben

Family beach trip, July 2014 with Uncle Chad, Aunt Lauren, cousin John Paul, Fella, Gabby, Bailey Grace, Ally, and dad and mom of course

Enjoying the fall leaves on our back porch, Ally (in the glasses) and Bailey Grace

CHAPTER 10

ON NOT BEING CONSUMED IN LIGHT OF HIS MERCIES

End of April, 2014

"Because of the Lord's great love we are not consumed,
for His compassions never fail. They are new every
morning; great is Your faithfulness."

—LAMENTATIONS 3:22–23

I LOVE THE PSALMS, AND I love David for his emotional tangents in them. One second, he is saying God has forsaken him and that life is horrible; the next, he is reminding himself and others that God is, in fact, good and that his joy is found in that. I can more than relate. After the girls' birthday party, it didn't take me long to go from the mountain of joy to the depths of despair. The Israelites in the Old Testament give a wonderful representation of this rebellion in all of our hearts. It seemed as if their crying out to God only occurred whenever they felt helpless or were in a pinch. Once things got comfortable, they were prone to turning away once again. While we would all like to think we would have done differently in their shoes our lives tell otherwise. During many seasons of my life, I was totally connected with the Israelites in that when things were happy or going seemingly well, God was not exactly on the forefront of my brain. Sure, I might offer up a blessing before meals or read a quick devotional in the morning, but my steps and my moments were not directed toward seeing His face and allowing Him to live out His glories through my life. Throughout this journey with our babies, I had been all too aware that I needed Him in every moment, so while rebellion had not necessarily been my go-to, the roller coaster of emotions described in the psalms most certainly had. Around the time the girls turned one, I was almost 100 percent content with where we were, just living in the moment, trusting God with whatever timing He had for us concerning answers. No more than a week later, I had become antsy to know more—consumed.

For most of my life, I had a tendency to focus on the second portion of Lamentations 3:22. The "His compassions never fail." After all, particularly in the seasons of life I would call lukewarm (at best), hearing that I knew a God who would never stop showing me pity in the midst of my sin relieved me. While I am no less sinful now, and it still certainly makes me feel good to have this knowledge, I have come to find much comfort in the first phrase of the sentence: "Because of the Lord's great love we are not consumed."

Not consumed. Dear reader, can you relate to this at all? What consumes you? What fills your mind and attention? What absorbs you, in a sense? In different seasons of my life, I can look back and recognize different things that took most of my attention. There have been varying degrees of consumption, but the one common thread that ties them together is self. Self-consumption. Self-centeredness. The truth is, the more wrapped up I have gotten in myself, the more miserable I tended to become. In a practical sense, thinking about your own problems and feeling sorry for oneself never gets you anywhere. The trial stays the same; the circumstance isn't altered by your thoughts. I have found that the more I think about myself, my life, and me, the worse I feel. It only makes my own tribulations look bigger. But what do we do when it seems as if our own problems are glaring us in the face and we can't seem to get past them? What do we do when as hard as we try, our own stuff just won't seem to get off the forefront of our brains? Jesus. .

In the in-between season in which I continued to wait for answers, each day I woke up and had to make a choice of whether or not I let my mind focus on getting answers or simply God. It was a choice that some days, I was wiser in than others. But you know what? I was never disappointed when I chose God. I was never let down when I allowed Him to penetrate my mind rather than the things I thought were being withheld from me. The truth is, He promises us that He withholds no good thing from us (Psalm 84:11). In light of this, us not having a diagnosis was God's best for our life. I could choose to believe this, to cling to God and the truth He offers or I could get so caught up in what I thought was more important that I would quickly lose sight of the eternal. Psalm 119:20 says, "My soul is consumed with longing for Your rules at all times."

David was consumed all right, but what consumed him did not bring him to despair, but rather to hope. You see, because of the Lord's great love for us, we truly do not have to be consumed by anything less than Him. No affliction, no present suffering, is greater than His unfailing, never-giving-up love. Because of Christ, we are freed up to be consumed with the things of heaven. It sounds easy, but what does that look like? At one point, I thought that meant thinking about halos, clouds, and bowing down all the time. Now I believe that God is simply asking us to be consumed with the things that don't perish, the things that will last through all eternity. Him. You see, that's the risk of being consumed with self: not only is it futile, but it is passing. The troubles of yesterday may or may not be the troubles of today. They aren't worth our time because at some point, no matter what you believe, they are going away. The things of God, His Word and His love, last. When I got so fixated on comparing how hard our life was in light of someone else's, I was brought to despair. When I thought of Christ and the hope and purpose He brings, the fog was lifted, and I felt free. The thing is this: we are right in thinking that there may be people around us suffering less; but as I have said before, for every person that suffers less, you can find someone who has suffered more. Beyond that, in comparison to Christ and how He suffered for us, all our trials are rags. Because of His death on the cross, we are promised that all tribulations are light and momentary but serve an eternal purpose. Furthermore the purpose of our suffering is to make us more like Christ, not more likely to be bitter at the cup in our hands. It is to make us more compassionate for those around us, not to formulate our own measuring stick of comparison in which we determine who is suffering more. The relieving part is this: we are not left in our own strength to follow through with this. We have Christ as the example, who said, "Yet not my will but Yours be done" (Luke 22:42). This is not some altruistic, "You will feel better if you get your mind off of yourself and onto others" kind of thinking. That may work sometimes, but in times of immense pain and heartache, we need something tried and true, something that lasts. Christ has given us the freedom to look not on our own lot, but to put it in His hands and trust Him to do the rest and to fix our eyes on the unseen rather than the seen.

So, friends, I ask you again. The lessons the Lord was teaching us are not just for our family, but for you as well. What consumes you? Is it that nagging health problem that just won't go away? That name brand dress you don't have the money for but just really have to have? Your sports team and the upcoming season? Work? Politics? The thing your spouse does that drives you crazy? The things you feel you lack? Your children? Singleness? Alcohol? Food? The list goes on and on, and only you and the Lord know what truly fills your mind. My encouragement to us all today is that we would choose to be consumed with God Himself. That we would look to heaven with an attitude of trust and gratitude, confident that whatever He has given us is His absolute best. He is worthy.

Lessons Learned

* Do you find yourself feeling more connected to God in the seemingly hard times or the seemingly easy times? Why do you think that is?
* As the author asks, what consumes you? What fills your mind and gets your attention the most?
* Why should we strive to be consumed with God and His Word and not the things of this world?

CHAPTER 11

WE WAIT FOR WHAT?

May 2014

"But I will sing of Your strength; I will sing aloud of Your steadfast
love in the morning. For You have been to me a fortress and a refuge
in the day of my distress. O my Strength, I will sing praises to You, for
You, O God, are my fortress, the God who shows me steadfast love."

—PSALM 59: 16–17

WAITING. NONE OF US LIKE to do it. In the American culture, we are not forced to wait on much, and we are all prone to get impatient at a rapid pace if we have to do so. We live in a world of fast food, quick marts, express, and go; the idea of waiting on anything produces anxiety and frustration in us all. So much of it falls back on the lack of control that ensues during the wait; much of it is associated with our own selfish desires and time tables. What is the first thing we do when we find ourselves in a traffic jam? After huffing and puffing about the fact that we are going to be late to the place we are intending to go, we then frantically try and figure out what is going on and how long it is going to be until the traffic dissipates and life continues on as planned. Our schedule. Our time line. Seemingly little incidents like this happen to us often and serve as a great reminder that life does not revolve around us, but what happens when it isn't just a detour on the highway? What happens when we are the one in the head-on collision? When the cancer comes back? When death comes suddenly? When the baby prayed for isn't? When your job is no longer yours? When we are stopped in our tracks by the life that God chose for us that is drastically different than the life we foresaw? It is then that we can sometimes find ourselves paralyzed in the waiting, frozen in the unknown.

I have always craved knowledge, not just in a scholastic sense. As I child, I became fixated on the connection between God and dinosaurs, and read book after book on the topic. I watched the weather channel for hours and read encyclopedias that would normally just collect dust on the bookshelves. Why? I just wanted to know. When I would try out for a sports team or play, I would spend the moments between when I tried out and when I was told the results obsessing over the whole thing and analyzing whether or not I thought I had made it. It wasn't necessarily that I cared much about the results; it was more about just knowing the outcome.

Around the middle of May, we found out that the last known diagnosis we were waiting to get results from was negative. We then sent off more blood work and began the six month wait to see what rarer, rare diagnosis they might discover. The chances that they would figure it out were relatively high, but the likelihood that we would be two of a handful of people with that diagnosis, without much of a prognosis, was equally probable. Six months wait to find out blurry information? Sounded like this knowledge seeker's nightmare. But God.

As I prayed through that new chapter in our family's journey, the Lord spoke to the depths of my soul concerning the unknowns. In all authenticity, I had the tendency to look at others' life stories and question. Why did they have a diagnosis? Why did they find out so quickly? I wasn't asking God to take it all away (although at times that might have been nice!); I was simply asking for an explanation of some kind. If only I could have a support group of moms who were walking the same road…if only we could have had a slight idea of what the future would look like for our family…if only…

Patient and merciful as He is, God brought me to the pages of His word, and I was nourished and refreshed by the truth that I was in good company. After all, the Bible is full of people who have walked moments, hours, even years of waiting for the unknown. Noah built an ark while the sun was still shining. Abraham went to a country that he didn't know and then offered up his son without awareness that God was not going to make him follow through with the sacrifice. The Israelites crossed over the Red Sea without the assurance that it wouldn't swallow them up. David and Goliath, Daniel and the lions' den, and the list goes on and on with story after story of those who trusted without borders. How? They were comfortable with an unknown circumstance in light of a known God. The best part is this: the Lord says that "...all these, though commended through their faith, did not receive what was promised, since God had provided something better for us, that apart from us they should not be made perfect" (Hebrews 11:39). Apart from us. Apart from your story, my story. All things are being tied together in light of what we are truly waiting for—our Savior and the moment when, as He sees fit, He unites His children with Himself and the trials are finished for good. No more waiting; no more wandering in the desert of the unknown. One with Him forever. The truth is, we are all waiting on that which we cannot see. How light and momentary these seasons of waiting will seem in light of the One who is more than worth our wait. What you wait for, what I wait for, is not a diagnosis. It isn't a husband, or more money, or another job. It is not five pounds lost. It isn't a baby or physical healing on this side of heaven for loved ones or ourselves. It's Him.

No matter what those next six months brought, I was determined to find my hope and expectation in the liberation of knowing that He could set me free from idolizing an answer and I could truly gain independence from desiring the knowledge that comes from that which fades. That is my prayer for you as well, dear reader. He is our Ultimate Answer. We are watching and waiting for Him and Him alone (Psalm 59:9). Let it be known that He holds us all in the palm of His hand, and knowledge of that will always trump any false security a diagnosis might bring. I pray that

He empresses this truth firmly in your heart today: your hope is not found in that which fades and changes. Your hope is found in Love Himself who holds the keys to every chapter of the book of the life He has given you. With Him, the last sentence is always "happily ever after for eternity." A miracle had begun in me that only God Himself could have performed: I was beginning to see that maybe the in-between was the bigger part of the story after all. Maybe His glory was being most seen in the midst of what felt like silence. Maybe I wasn't waiting on a diagnosis. Maybe, just maybe, I was simply waiting on Him.

Lessons Learned

- What do you find yourself waiting for in this particular time of life? Has the waiting been easy or hard? Why?
- Why do you think we become fearful or frustrated in the midst of the unknown?
- Would you want to know all the details of your life, today? Why or why not?
- Why do you think that, at times, God withholds some details from us?

CHAPTER 12

EVERYTHING SHE HAD

⟨⁓

May 2014

"O Lord, my heart is not lifted up; my eyes are not raised too high;
I do not occupy myself with things too great and too
marvelous for me. But I have calmed and quieted my soul,
like a weaned child is my soul within me. O Israel, hope
in the Lord from this time forth and forevermore."

—PSALM 131

SOMETHING THAT WAS CERTAINLY CHALLENGING during this season of life
was making it to church, especially when Hugh was working. We were
unable to take the girls to the nursery, simply because of the risk of germs
and illness that came with having them in a class with so many other children. At that point, our best option was to sit in the back and hope they
would not distract us (or those around us!) too much. For couples with
children who have special needs, being able to worship with one another is
crucial for a marriage that is being so stretched daily; and Hugh and I were
determined to be able to do so. One particular Sunday in May, I knew that
Hugh and I would not make it to our regular 6:00 p.m. church service, so
I attempted to take the girls to the 11:00 a.m. Technically Ally and Bailey
Grace nap then and eat right after, so I knew this was going to be a stretch.

A seemingly single mom waking into church with a stroller equivalent to a double wide might as well be a three-man circus. There were lots of sympathetic smiles, rushing to open the door as if I'm coming in with a Mack truck, and many "oohs" and "ahhs." I was pretty sure we were not going to make it through the entire service, but I needed to be able to be filled with His presence and be close to His people for at least a little bit. When we were home, Bailey Grace and Ally tended to be relatively interactive, smiling, and content. For reasons that we could not understand (maybe extra stimulation and new things?), they often seemed to freeze when we were out in public. It was like a light switch had been turned off at times, and to be honest, it frustrated me because I wanted people to be able to engage with our sweet girls and see them as they truly were. When the first praise song began, I glanced over and saw Ally kicking her legs to the music. God spoke to my heart with such clarity in that moment: This is the kind of praise I desire. She is bringing all she has without reservation. In that moment, Ally wasn't worried about whether her gift to God was silly, whether she was kicking to the beat, or what her gift was compared to those around her. She just brought what she could. For girls that were unable to sit, much less move, how sweet it was that it was the very thing she chose to offer. During this waiting, our girls were teaching me such valuable lessons on how the Lord saw me and those around me; lessons that would last in a deeply eternal way.

God's Word also gives a beautiful account of a woman who chose to give all she had to contribute. Mark 12:41–44 says as follows:

And He (Jesus) sat down opposite the treasury and watched the people putting money into the offering box. Many rich people put in large sums. And a poor widow came and put in two small copper coins, which make a penny. And He called His disciples to Him and said to them, "Truly, I say to you, this poor widow has put in more than all those who are contributing to the offering box. For they all contributed out of their abundance, but she out of her poverty has put in everything she had, all she had to live on." (emphasis mine)

Because of the cross and what Jesus did for those of us who have faith to believe, we no longer have to sacrifice animals for our sins. While God does not need anything from us, for He is ruler over all, He gives us the privilege of showing Him our love in different ways. Time, money, and the talents He has given us are some of those ways. Romans 14:7 reminds us that we are not our own masters; therefore, how we spend our time is not up to us once we have made Christ our Lord. Matthew 6:24 exhorts us that we cannot love God and money, so the way that we spend the money God has entrusted us is up to Him. Romans 12:6–8 states that we have all been given different gifts and talents and that God desires to use those for good. Ultimately we are called to offer the Gospel to all, as 1 Peter 3:15 commands us. These are all great things to offer, but how often do we find ourselves offering up the easiest thing? We have plenty of money, so we give out of our abundance so that someone else can go spend their time in another country. We enjoy serving, so we offer our time and trust that someone who lives more comfortably than us will give financially. We find it easy to teach the preschool class, so we do that, but feel no need to share the Gospel because evangelism doesn't come easily for us. These are just a few examples, but I want to encourage us all to give where it is uncomfortable. Do the very thing that doesn't come naturally to you because it is there God will meet you, and your dependence on Him to show up will grow. This is where faith is stretched and molded.

Beyond that, I believe that the New Testament reminds us that it is the very things of the heart that He is most pleased. Hebrews 13:15 says, "Through Him then let us continually offer up a sacrifice of praise to God, that is the fruit of lips that acknowledge His name." Don't miss the first part. Through Him. When tragedy strikes, whatever that looks like in your life, He gives you the ability to praise Him in the midst. It is Him who turns despair and darkness into hope and light. Praise *is* a sacrifice sometimes. When things are going as we planned, saying, "God is good," is not that difficult and does not require much faith. When everything around appears to be crumbling, when we are absolutely stripped of the comforts of this world, He is most pleased when we choose to praise

Him instead of shaking our fists at the sky and asking, "Why?' We offer a sacrifice of praise because we know He can be trusted. As we look at generations past and look at the ways He has loved us and those around us, we know that He is most worthy of our affections and our worship, Sometimes the sacrifice of our praise, of our trust, or of our contentment in the season He has placed us in is our way of offering up everything we have in that moment. It is not easy. It can be most painful, in fact. But isn't that what sacrifice is—offering something precious to us for the sake of something greater? Let's look at the example of our Savior who sacrificed not only His life, but also gave everything so that our imperfect slate could be forever wiped clean. Eternally with Him. Why? Because it was worth it to Him. Pleasing His Father in heaven was worth it. You were worth it. Let that sink in today. And whatever your sacrifice may be, whether it is the tiny kicks of your legs to the music or your very life, bring it.

Lessons Learned

* Do you offer up what is convenient or do you offer up that which is more challenging? What is easiest for you to offer up (examples: time, money, words of affirmation, or gifts of service)? What is hardest?
* Have you ever thought about praise as a sacrifice? When and why? Give an example of a time that you or someone you love offered up a sacrifice of praise.
* What can you offer up to the Lord today, in gratitude, that you might have been holding on to too tightly?

CHAPTER 13

CRY NO MORE

⟨ ⟩

"Arise, cry out in the night, at the beginning of the night
watches! Pour out your heart like water before the presence
of the Lord! Lift your hands to Him for the lives of your
children, who faint for hunger at the head of every street."

—LAMENTATIONS 2:19

"Jesus wept."

—JOHN 11:35

I HAVE NOT ALWAYS BEEN a crier. Sure I would shed a tear or two in a movie theater every now and then, and there were a couple of breakups that felt dramatically tearful at the time, but I never really had much to cry about growing up. As sheltered as that sounds, I was never moved to tears by much. The more I got to know the Lord and what He had done for me, and once I fell in love with my husband and actually allowed myself to be in a position to hurt, the tears began to flow. Once those walls were broken down, I found myself crying about nearly anything. A commercial, a sad or extra happy story, or really anything that invited emotion brought water to my eyes and passion to my soul. Most of those tears, however, were not brought about by immense pain.

The intensity of the emotions that I felt during the first year and a half of the girls' lives was unlike anything I had ever experienced. For those of you that are parents, you know the reality that is experienced when you hold your child for the first time. That terrified feeling I had while holding the girls in that NICU room was all based on the intense emotions that I was feeling. After that, the pain that I felt seemed insurmountable at times. While I always wanted to make sure others knew that Christ was sustaining us, I never wanted to portray that it was void of normal human pain and emotion. We are not superhuman. Far from it. We have a super God who continues to carry us but at times, our life can feel heart-wrenching. How do you begin to process walking into a neurology appointment in which you could potentially be told both of your children have a life-threatening disease? How do you walk through days of being told that something is "not right" with your children, while also being informed that no one has any idea of what it is or what it will entail? When our girls got sick, my anxiety would reach the roof. Because we did not know what was causing the girls' hypotonia, we were also not positive what systems of their bodies were being affected. When they got a cough, their low tone caused them to have a hard time clearing secretions, and we often lived in fear of all the "what ifs" involved. Every day, I would look at our almost thirteen-month-old girls who struggled to grab a toy that wasn't right nearby, who tried as they might to sit up but shook and fell right back down, and my eyes would sting with tears. I would sometimes lie awake wondering how in the world I would be able to push two wheelchairs around if that was the Lord's plan in our girls' lives and if there was even a van big enough for that task in the first place. While we were hopeful that it might not be our reality, and while we knew the Lord had already seen the future and was planning ahead for us, we are human, and this is the reality of where we were some days. I am laughing and crying as I admit that when we went to the gym or nursery (places where other kids would be), I would always make sure the girls were dressed their absolute best. They may not have been able to play with the other kids, but were going to look adorable. Often when I left these places, I held it together until I got in the car and then the tears would fall. Like every parent, I just wanted to save the girls from any and all hurt. The truth is that the girls could have cared less. Ally and Bailey Grace embody the fruits of the Spirit unlike any I have met before, and they have always made it obvious that they think their lives are the absolute greatest. I am the one who, if I am authentic, spent many days feeling as if the reality of our situation stuck a knife in the depths of my heart. I do not tell you these things for a pity party. God has saved us and is planning for us more than we could possibly imagine. You cannot live on this planet without walking through hard things, and I know so many others who live the challenging day to day as well. However, I want to make it clear that just because we know and serve a powerful God who is carrying us doesn't mean we don't feel the weight of our circumstances at times.

On a particularly heavy Sunday morning in which I felt burdened by the weight of the story He was writing, our pastor mentioned the verses in Psalms in which the Lord reminds us that He has kept count of our tossings and that He puts our tears in a bottle (Psalm 56:8). This was comforting to me and then I remembered that in Revelations, He also says that there will be no more tears in heaven (Revelations 21:4). So if He has this bottle of my tears, but it is not in heaven, where was it? When Jesus comes back again, is He going to make this so-called bottle appear so that I can know it actually existed, but make it disappear at the exact same time?

The Lord revealed a beautiful truth to me that morning. I believe that the reason we will never see this bottle is because God, in His wisdom and might, is making something out of that bottle of tears that is bringing Him the glory and us all things good. As the tears fall, He is collecting them in order to create something precious that far surpasses the emotions that brought about the tears in the first place. The best part is that He doesn't have tear criteria. He doesn't say that only certain tears make the cut. He carefully and intricately cares about each and every one of them. One day in heaven, He will present me, present you, with something that is indescribably beautiful that could have only been crafted with each of the tears that streamed down. Your pain and crying is for a purpose. It is a vital and important piece of your story, and one day, it will be more than worth it. Whatever you are walking through today, I encourage you to trust Him with the weight of the story He is writing in your life. There is a season for everything (Ecclesiastes 3), and sometimes He brings laughter. When He does, let the belly laughs come. But when He allows pain, let the tears fall, confident that He is collecting them for something beyond what you could have asked for or dreamed up. He cares. He loves us. He is always working for His glory and our good. Be encouraged today that not one tear will be wasted in His kingdom. Rejoice in the fact that once He calls you home, He promises you an eternity of no more crying. Thanks be to God and God alone! Only He can turn our mourning into dancing. I left that Sunday morning with a renewed confidence in His plans for our family's life; refreshed with the comfort only He could have provided.

Lessons Learned

- When is the last time you cried and why?
- How does it make you feel to know that God cares about each one of your tears? How does it make you feel to know that tears of sadness will not exist in heaven?
- Do you believe that God has a reason for each of your tears? How does this comfort you today in whatever you are walking through? Be specific.

CHAPTER 14

WAITING ON ONE

June 2014

"If the Lord Jehovah makes us wait, let us do so with our whole hearts; for blessed are all they that wait for Him. He is worth waiting for. The waiting itself is beneficial to us; it tries faith, exercises patience, trains submission, and endears the blessing when it comes. The Lord's people have always been a waiting people."

—CHARLES SPURGEON

A COMMON THEME IN THE story of our family's life was this concept of waiting. As I spoke in Chapter 11, I spent much of the girls' first year of life simply waiting on answers. Beyond that, as the waiting continued, I realized that this idea of waiting seems so implicatively negative in our society. In God's Word, God speaks of waiting with hope. In the world we live in, waiting certainly does not have great connotations. To say we are waiting on something tends to imply that the condition or state we are in is going to improve once said thing arrives. We don't like to wait to be seated in a restaurant, sometimes because we are hungry and other times simply because we just want a table immediately. We want what we want and when we want it. Taking it a step further, many of us might verbalize that we are in a season of waiting. Often this is correlated with a season of life. It seems as if we are always in anticipation for the next season, whatever it might be. In singleness, for dating. In dating, for engagement. In engagement, for marriage. In marriage, for children. With children, we are either waiting until they get out of the house so we can be an empty-nester or we are wondering what we will do once we finally reach that destination. Other times, we are a people who wait for the next thing on our calendar. Whether it is for a friend's wedding, for tax season to be over, for residency to be finished, for the chemotherapy to stop, for five more pounds to come off, for our husband to come back from Afghanistan, for more money to come in, or for the results to come back in, we wait. But for what?

Waiting can be defined as this: to stay where one is or delay action until something else happens or a particular time occurs. I have done this in so many different ways at various times in life, and I would certainly describe this time in the same way. I am waiting. Waiting for a diagnosis is what I would tell you. But for what?

Here is the thing: the feeling in our hearts that urges us to look for something else, something better, is absolutely God-given. We were not meant to be satisfied with the here and now, so the desire for something more is not wrong in the least. The problem with how we tend to wait is that we wait on something temporary that is going to continue to leave us longing. I love my husband, and I cannot imagine a better partner to walk beside through this life. However, I wish I could have told my single, dating, and engaged self this concrete truth: Stop waiting for the next thing to come. Enjoy where you are because you are going to look back and realize how wonderful it actually was. To my single readers, marriage is great. There are many perks, and I wouldn't trade it for the world. However, it is not where life is found. Particularly as women, I think we idolize marriage as a state in which we will feel most secure. I remember thinking that so much sin and temptation would disappear once I got married, but it is actually quite the opposite. As a married person, I know it is easy to give out words of wisdom after the fact, but I truly exhort you to trust me that whether you ever get married or not, you will not reach some different level of satisfaction once you do. I digress.

Concerning other matters, I think experience is, in fact, the best teacher. Think about all the things that you have spent time waiting on. As a child, I remember thinking that if I could only get a dog, life would be perfect. I gave my parents a serious binder, full of pages on why it was reasonable for us to get a dog (maybe I should have been a lawyer). Finally they agreed. Having a dog was great for a while, but guess what? It didn't take long for the luster to wear off (and we had to give him to another family fairly quickly...another story for another day!). Isn't that how everything tends to work? As teenagers, we look forward to prom, only to have an OK time. We all spend time preparing for holidays, celebrations, parties, and other events, and no matter how great of a time we have, it is over in the blink of an eye, and we are left the same as before—waiting for the next thing.

Because we continued to sit in a season of wanting answers, I feel the need to go back to God's Word and His desires for us in our waiting. I, like the Israelites, was all too familiar with grasping onto the truths of God's Word only to doubt them yet again; which is seen so clearly on the pages of this book. I include this back and forth dynamic longing for you as the reader to find hope in following another sinner's path to freedom. So often, we (Christians) desire to show the world the Christ in us while hiding the flesh and its tendencies. Our path of sanctification is messy; and the victory is not always seen in the immediate. I pray that this is experienced as you walk with me through this particular season of life. During that time, a part of me felt like receiving a diagnosis was all I needed to move forward in our family's life. While this might have been partially true, I began to beg my heart to process the truth that a diagnosis would not truly change anything. If there was a day on this side of heaven that we found out what was going on with our sweet girls, that day would start out and end just like any other—still left wanting for something more. The Word of God talks a lot about waiting, but it only fixes our souls on one thing:

waiting on the Lord. Why? God Himself knows that when we put our hope in anything else, we will not be filled. Psalm 130:5 puts it this way: "We wait for the Lord, my soul waits, and in His word I put my hope."

Isaiah 30:8, Romans 8:23, Hebrews 9:28, and 1 Thessalonians 1:10 echo a similar cry. If there is anything worth waiting for, it is Him. All other things will pass and fade away. Anything else we are waiting on, however seemingly glorious, is rags in comparison to what will happen to our souls and bodies when we see Him face-to-face. I recognize this doesn't change the emotions or hardships that come when we are waiting on something, albeit temporary, that we desire. *And, Morgan,* some of you are thinking, *God promises me He will give me the desires of my heart, and He hasn't yet.* Yes, friend, this is a promise in His word. But do not miss this part: "Delight yourself in the Lord and He will give you the desires of your heart" (Psalm 37:4). The amazing thing about life is this: when we are delighting in the Lord, His desires become our desires. So if He does not grant us the thing we wish for, we recognize this not as a desire unmet but as a prayer answered from God, in His wisdom, who knows best and who will withhold no good thing from those who love Him (Psalm 84:11). As we delight ourselves in the Lord, the desires of our hearts change, and we simply desire that which He places in our hands. No more waiting. As we spend our time focused on Him and the things He *has* placed in front of us, a beautiful thing happens—he puts a *new* song in our mouths while we wait! It is a new song that doesn't demand its own wants but that trusts in Him and praises Him for whatever lies behind, presently, and ahead (Psalm 40:1). This cannot happen, however, if we are constantly fixated on the next big thing or the thing we think we should have now.

In light of this truth, I began to realize that I was simply over waiting. Yes, I would have been grateful if God chose to give us a diagnosis. I would have been thankful if His plan included us gaining that knowledge, and I prayed for it every single day. But, instead of focusing on the answers I thought I wanted, I began to choose to trust that there was nothing He was withholding from me; therefore, waiting for anything less than Jesus Christ Himself was futile, fruitless, and fleeting. Life was not found in a diagnosis. Life was not found in anything outside of Him. I wanted to spend my life living, not waiting.

I don't know what you are walking through exactly, but I do know that chances are, you are waiting on something. Whether it is as seemingly simple as a ring on your finger or as heavy as a lab result that could change what you intended your future to look like, I urge you to stop waiting. The plan is His regardless of it we choose to let go or not. Let's live in the present, focus on what makes our hearts joyful today, and choose to wait expectantly on Him and Him alone.

Lessons Learned

* At any particular season of life (maybe the one you are in now!), have you found yourself believing the lie that "the next thing" would satisfy you? If it was a time in the past, what do you wish that you knew then, now?
* Read Psalm 130:5. Are you a woman who ultimately waits on the Lord? If not, what is it that you find yourself waiting on most?
* How can we encourage one another to wait on the Lord instead of the things of this world? Give practical examples for the week ahead.

CHAPTER 15
CONSUMED YET AGAIN

⌒

June 2014

"...their strength is to sit still."

—Isaiah 30:7b (King James Bible)

Oh, the humanity of it all. As soon as I thought I had conquered this struggle of being consumed with desiring answers, it felt like I was back in the same place yet again. One summer evening, Hugh and I decided to go out to dinner with the girls. This was not something we did often during that season, both for the sake of the challenges it entailed and also because of the insecurities of all the questions that tended to arise from others. After devouring some local Chinese cuisine (one of our favorites), we walked back to our car, car seats in hand, and a man rolled down his window.

"Twins?" he asked. *What a dumb question*, I thought to myself.

"Yes, sir," I pleasantly responded back.

"I have twins!" he proudly yelled back. "How old are yours?" Hugh and I gave each other the awkward look we always do when this question comes up, and I quickly sputtered back, "14 months or so," as I put Bailey Grace in the car, hoping he would get the hint.

"Walking yet?" This one was relentless.

"Not yet," Hugh responded before I could give my unfiltered response.

"Once they start that, it gets even crazier. But it gets easier and easier, so don't worry." Hugh and I fake laughed and got in our car, both silent for a few minutes.

"You know," I started, "It makes me so mad when people give us that line. He has no idea what we are going through. He has no idea that for us, it's not going to get easier. He just doesn't get it." As these words came out of my mouth, I flashed back to my conversation with a dear client from years past. I remembered it as if it were yesterday...

I walked into her trailer for what could have been the fiftieth time in the past few years, but this time, her eyes were inverted down. I quickly looked around to see if there was something I was missing in her home—a new man, perhaps, that I had caught her in the act with or some kind of afternoon substance fix she forgot to cover up. I saw nothing and then she looked up. The bruises on her arms she could cover up. The black eye she could not. Layers of pain and hurt from years of protecting herself from feeling anything prevented her from letting even a single tear flow, but the hurt in my heart caused me to blink mine back in an effort to stay somewhat professional.

"Pamela*," I started to say, searching for some kind of words. "You know..." the words trailed off as Pamela cut in.

"Ms. Morgan, you can stop. You don't understand what my life has been like. You don't get what I go through every day. Just don't even try to give me some positive soap box because I already have enough bullshit in my life, OK?"

Five years later, I stood in that Chinese restaurant parking lot pouring out those same emotions to my husband. While my pain and Pamela's pain were so different, it came from such a similar place. Both of us, so caught up in our own stuff, so consumed, that we could not see outside of our own circumstances. I began to realize that sometimes, our consummation has to do with the things we desire that we feel are being withheld; and other times, we get so caught up in our own perspective that we cannot take the lenses of self off. At times, we throw pity parties that stem directly from thinking our neighbor has it better. While Pamela and I might have handled our situations a litle differently, my heart was in the exact place hers was in that moment: I was allowing the enemy to bring me to a place of isolation of heart; and I was refusing to believe in that moment that God's plans for me as an individual were good. I was sick of waiting for God to come through in the ways that I thought were best. I would have never worded it that way, yet my anger and bitterness toward the man in the parking lot made it so. Sometimes, our actions truly do speak louder than our words; and mine were blantantly clear that afternoon.

As we pulled away and I flashed forward to the present, I initially felt shame for the bitterness that had crept up out of my heart, and then later felt relief. I realized that the God of the universe had the power to handle all my consummations, even the ugliest of ugly. His death on the cross covered both Pamela's hurts and my own. He was teaching me humility and trust out of the very nature of the season of life He had us in, and while painful, it was a lesson that would bring me to a love and compassion for those around me that I could have not learned otherwise. We are all so human, but thanks be to God for the immeasurable gifts of grace found in Jesus. As I reveled in these truths that night, I had no idea what was around the corner and the endurance and new grace He was about to provide our family.

Jesus.
*Name changed for privacy

Lessons Learned

- When do you find yourself most tempted to throw a "pity party"?
- What situations or conversations make you struggle with jealousy or comparison the most? Why do you think that is?
- What do you think God wants us to be consumed with today? Why do you think He desires this for us?

CHAPTER 16

ON PAIN AND THE HOSPITAL

End of June 2014, a compliation of our first hospital stay with the girls
"Though He slay me, yet I will hope in Him."

—JOB 13:15

"God, who foresaw your tribulation has specifically armed
you to go through it, not without pain but without stain."

—C. S. LEWIS

PAIN. WE CANNOT AVOID IT, and we all dislike it. Whether physical or emotional, pain takes a toll on not only us, but on those around us as well. I have always been told God whispers in our pleasures and shouts in our pain (C. S. Lewis), and that reality became all the more clear at the end of June. The girls seemed to have developed a bad cold one week, and Bailey Grace in particular was showing signs of distress. She was not drinking much at all, and when she did, she would cough so violently that she would vomit. After a full day of not getting her to drink anything without throwing up, combined with the fact that she seemed dehydrated and was breathing pretty heavily, I knew that it was time to take her in to the hospital. The dynamics at our house can get interesting with Hugh being in pediatrics, especially when he is not at home to give his own evaluation. With the report I was giving, he discerned we should take her to the after-hours clinic, and he let me know he would meet me there. I am so thankful we made this choice.

When we brought Bailey Grace into the clinic, I had no idea where our week was headed. I am so thankful, for I think I might have crumbled under it all. I truly want this story to be about the Healer Himself, but it is important for me to give enough detail for you to comprehend where we were. Bailey Grace was very dehydrated, febrile, slightly tachycardic, and generally out of it. The after-hours team decided that we need to have Bailey Grace admitted to the special care unit. Now I know that I have said that there was an inkling in my head that we would be in this position at some point, but we had never thought out how to navigate the whole thing. At that moment, Ally was sick but not "hospital" sick, and Hugh was clearly supposed to work the next day. After realizing that we were going to have to split up, Hugh suggested that I go home to be with Ally. This was absolutely out of the question for me. Why? Because my child was in pain, and she needed me. I obviously love Ally as much as I do Bailey Grace, but in that moment, my heart was drawn to Bailey Grace because she was hurting the most. *He whispers in our pleasures, and shouts in our pain.* As I sat up with her, watching her moan and let out feeble cries of pain and discomfort that night, this truth hit me and left me speechless. This is what God does for me, for you. We always wonder where He is in our deepest pain and suffering. Friends, I am here to tell you that He is right by our bedside, holding our hand and loving us in the ways only He can.

That week quickly went from being a bad dream to a nightmare. Once Bailey Grace got better, we had one long night at home only to have to bring Ally to the ER. She was showing similar signs as Bailey Grace, and as much as we wanted to take a breather, we jumped right back into the hard. Things are always relative, and I didn't have to walk too far down the hallway to see that, but in that moment, there were points that I believed the lie that we were going to be crushed by it all. 2 Corinthians 4:8 says it best: "We are hard pressed on every side, but not crushed; perplexed, but not in despair."

Not crushed. Not in despair. This is His promise. Even when we feel like we are being smothered by the circumstance, His word promises we are not and that He will lift up our eyes to the hills once again. He is where our help comes from. During this hospital stay, there were many times I doubted this truth. When Bailey Grace began to cough up blood in the middle of the night and our nurse had gone on a break- *Lord, is this really your best for her?* When she moaned, coughed, and cried for two days straight- *Father, how am I supposed to trust you here?* When every nurse on the floor could not find a vain because she was so dehydrated, and my child was looking over at me, too weak to cry but writhing in pain-*Abba, this feels like too much to* handle. When we finally got her home, only to be up all night with her coughing and listless sister-*Now, God? Really?* When we took Ally to the ER, and they determined she needed to be admitted-*I can't Lord. I just can't.* When they continued to have to suction the mucus out of Ally's throat because she choked on it, too weak to cough it up. When she could not drink any fluids, and I wondered how many more hospital visits we might have to go through. I doubted. But you know what? That's OK. He was not concerned with my wavering faith because He knew His own strength. Friends, in our deepest pain and suffering, God is so very near. So often, we make the mistake of viewing Him through our own frailty. How quickly we boil Him down to our own ever-changing, sometimes deceptive emotions. He is the rescuer. The Savior. The Maker of all things. He is always acting, always working and never tires. He is absolutely right there with you, even when you don't have the strength to cry out. As I sat in the first hospital room, exhausted and unable to think after not sleeping any the first night of Bailey Grace's stay, my head pounded, and I simply could not focus on His Word. It wasn't up to me to make the Word come alive, however, and He did so for me even in the midst of my flesh and emotions absolutely failing me. Psalm 119:175 says, "Let my soul live and praise You, and let Your rules help me." In this life, we do not have to set the standard of our hearts and our emotions in order to find life because in so many things, they will absolutely leave us lacking (Psalm 73:25). Instead we must remember that our ultimate prayer is for our soul to know life and for the depths of who we are to trust His life to be lived out in ours. This is the only place that we can truly live. I was so very weak in my flesh that week in June, and honestly, who wouldn't be? Look at the circumstances: little to no sleep, emotionally drained, miserably sick babies, lots of unknowns, roller coaster of health, helplessness in taking care of my little ones, out of the hospital for one night only to be admitted again the next. But God. He shouted to my soul to come alive and friends, it was well with my soul. Truly. He continued to shout in the midst of gut-wrenching pain, and I know that no matter what you are walking through today, He promises to do the same for you. He will fight for you. You need only be still (Exodus 14:14). He does not compare His children, and the strength and grace He offers to each of us is limitless and not based on another. He wants to be your wisdom. He desires to be your strength. He simply loves you in all the brokenness and all the mess because you are His child. The presence of pain does not lessen the reality of His love for us; it strengthens it.

Once we were home, it was tempting to look to the fact that a simple cold put the girls in danger to the point of hospitalization, and feel fearful. I could choose to live worried, or I could choose to look past the circumstances and look to the might of my unchanging God. He is the same in all things. He was not surprised by that week, and He promises He is working all things together for the kingdom, the one who truly matters. Friends, this world is not our home. This world is *not* our home. One day, He will not have to shout in our pain because pain will no longer exist when we see Him face-to-face. Whatever you are walking through today, He will give you what you need for the day as you look to Him to do so. What a mighty God we serve!

Lessons Learned

* As C. S. Lewis is quoted saying, do you believe God whispers in our pleasures and shouts in our pain? When has this been true in your life?
* How does it make you feel to know that God longs to be close to His children when they are hurting?
* The author says, "The presence of pain does not lessen the reality of His love for us; it strengthens it." What do you think about this? How have you seen this as true in your life?

CHAPTER 17

ON BEAUTY

June 2014

I almost took this chapter out, simply because it felt somewhat out of place.. I kept it here, however, because I believe that each of the lessons God teaches us have value. None of them are random, and He has a way of tying them all together in the most beautiful manner. For whatever reason, these words were meant to stay.

"But the Lord said to Samuel, "Do not look on his appearance or on the height of his stature, because I have rejected him. For the Lord sees not as man sees: man looks on the outward appearance, but the Lord looks on the heart."

—1 Samuel 16:7

Self-care took an extreme back window whenever the girls were born. I am not proud of this, but truly, we were in survival mode and sometimes that survival did not include showers, much less make-up. Whenever the girls were admitted to the hospital, sleep and hygiene went from bad to worse. This was so ironic, coming from someone (me!) who had spent years and years trying to perfect this concept of beauty. Shortly after, God reminded me how He had changed my definition of beauty not only prior to the girls but also through their beautiful lives.

What is the most beautiful thing you have ever seen? Is it a person? A place? A moment? We are all drawn to that which is beautiful. We love to watch a sun set or rise, to see a waterfall at the top of a mountain, or to marvel at the starlit sky. Our country spends millions of dollars on products that promise to make us feel more beautiful. Society places such a strong emphasis on women being beautiful and on the priority of doing all we can to successfully be attractive. My definition of beauty has varied throughout the years. During my middle school, high school, and beginning college years, I would spend hours and a lot of money on buying products and clothes that I thought would make me feel pretty. I would look in the mirror over and over just to double check that I was satisfied with the reflection I saw. Let's not even start on the hundreds of Dairy Queen blizzards that I missed out on, all in the name of beauty. At the time, my definition of beautiful revolved around being thin and fashionable. The problem was that there was always someone thinner and always someone trendier. This was in a time before selfies and Instagram, and I am thankful for this because I cringe when I think about the egotistical, self-focused things I would have posted. Basing our beauty on the external is not only fleeting, it is also subjective. What you think is beautiful might be totally different than what I do. Those years were full of feelings of insecurity and certainly days of being consumed with self. Sadly, if we are honest, this is the reality of so many of our minds. We are so obsessed with being deemed beautiful without realizing we are fighting a losing battle when the focus is external. The thing is that the external always and forever fades. Money can buy us all the surgery, makeup, antiaging products, and outfits this world has to offer, but time always wins and when all those things are stripped away, our external appearance is always left wanting. We are fighting a losing battle.

In the first year or so of the girls' lives, my wardrobe consisted of sweatpants, yoga pants, and more sweatpants. I was usually found without an ounce of makeup on my face, and a big cup of creamer with a splash of coffee stayed in front of me at all times. To the world, somewhat of a mess. But you know what? It is a season I can honestly say I felt beautiful in. The reflection might have said otherwise, and if you looked at a before and after picture from a few years past, the damage had certainly been done; yet God had freed me up to know that my beauty was absolutely not based on me. You see, there is a kind of beauty that surpasses what others think of us and what the mirror reflects. There is something within us that is given room to bubble up when all else is stripped. I had a friend describe this new season of our family's life in that way, and I could not have agreed more. We had been stripped—of comfort. Of control. Of our own selfish desires. Of expectations. And I felt more beautiful than ever, free, and so very loved. Don't you see, friends? Beauty is not dependent on that which we see. Our beauty is intricately connected to how intimately we are tied to our Maker. I was learning to see beauty in the imperfection, beauty in the mess, because I saw all the more room for God to bring beauty from the ashes. I had seen it in my own life, and I had seen it in the lives of those around me.

At the end of the day, we all prefer the real thing. We don't want a generic, fake version of the truth. We want authenticity. In fact, we could all agree that we find something or someone beautiful when it appears effortless. When anything is forced, it becomes awkward and undesirable. That's the thing about beauty. What is beautiful in you is going to be different than what is beautiful in me, but one thing I can promise you is this: it has to come from the inside out. This isn't a one-size-fits-all mentality. No, this is all of us being made in the image of God and creatively designed by our Maker, and therefore possessing much worth. In Mark 14, Jesus and some of his friends were eating dinner when a woman came and poured a costly jar of ointment on Jesus's head. Some people at the table were appalled that she had done such a thing, claiming that she should have sold the ointment to give to the poor and that it was all a waste. Jesus could not disagree more. He said to the people: "Leave her alone. Why do you trouble her? She has done a beautiful thing to me...she has done what she could" (verses 7–8).

Jesus found beauty in the woman, not based on what she looked like but rather on her heart toward Him. After all, if God thought external beauty was important, don't you think He would have made Jesus Himself attractive? Isaiah 53:2 reminds us that there was no beauty in Jesus's appearance that should make Him desirable. The beauty people saw in Jesus was based solely on who He was, not what He looked like.

I can promise you this: you will never be comfortable in your own skin until you are comfortable in your own soul. There you will find a beauty that is unfading, that has nothing to do with you but all to do with the One whose image you were created in. My encouragement to you today is this: find what is beautiful in you and look for what is beautiful in those around you. It won't be found in your clothes, your body, your makeup, your job, your abilities, or your performance. Dig deeper. You might be surprised that it is often in the broken, messy, and wounded places that beauty is most magnificently displayed. You are made in His image, and He has made you oh so beautiful. Only He can make beautiful things out of dust. I pray that you see, like I was beginning to see, that the One who made us holds true beauty in the palm of His hands.

Lessons Learned

* What is the most beautiful thing you have ever seen? If in a group setting, take some time to listen and share with one another.
* How does God define beauty? Do you think you are beautiful? Whether the answer is yes or no, what are you basing this on?
* The author states, "You will never be comfortable in your own skin until you are comfortable in your own soul." How have you found this to be true in your life or in the life of those around you?
* Who is the most beautiful person you know? What makes this person beautiful to you?

CHAPTER 18

HE SHOWS UP

July 2014

"I am not alone, because the Father is with me."

—JOHN 16:32

A FEW WEEKS AFTER WE had recovered from our first hospital admissions, I had a weekend alone with Ally and Bailey Grace. Because of Hugh's schedule, we were used to him being gone a good bit; a night here and there or a longer-than-expected day were just a part of the life God has chosen for us. That being said, a Friday through Sunday shindig is not the normal, and usually I have back up help for weekends like that. The girls and I kept ourselves busy, and it went by fairly quickly, but I was ready to hug my man and hand him a baby by the time Sunday arrived. When he got home and was obviously not feeling well, not only was I bummed because I was ready for a break, but panic also set in as I quickly replayed the last time our family was sick (might I add it was only a few weeks before). We all remember how that went.

The week before, we had an appointment with a doctor that I had so looked forward to seeing. He was a top neuromuscular physician in the area, and I truly felt like he was going to be able to give us some answers, or at least leeway, going forward. There had been so much silence concerning diagnosis, but the girls' development was not progressing for the most part, and I was starting to feel antsy yet again. Not only did this doctor not have any ideas as to what was going on, but he dismissed my concerns and simply told me I needed to stop focusing on getting a diagnosis and start focusing on "getting my girls to move," as if it was my fault and as if there was something I could have done to change the ways things were going. My blood pressure rises today even as I type this because this hits so many insecurities that I have felt throughout this whole journey. As much as I knew that whatever was going on with our girls was not a direct correlation to me, I sometimes could slip into the mind-set that if I were a better mom, the girls would be able to do more. I prayed and fought against those emotions every single day, and so to hear a physician speak these words stung to my very core. I left that appointment and spent the coming days reminding myself that I had an Audience of One, reminding myself of God's sovereignty and His perfect plan in all things. I was feeling down to say the least, and we will now refer to this doctor as "the man who deserves grace as much as I do." I had a moment where I simply begged God for some relief. I have done this several times throughout this season, and He always seems to provide something unexpected but equally encouraging. This relief came in the form of an e-mail from the NIH's undiagnosed program. Insert numerous God connections, and a week or so later, we had been accepted into their current research study. They only agree to work with fifty to one hundred families per year, and so you can imagine my excitement that our family was included on that list. While I knew that God was God and man was not, and that we could still end up without a diagnosis if that was what the Lord chose, I also knew that I would be much more at peace accepting that after "the best of the best" reviewed our case. We were left with a few months to wait, and possible travel involved, but I was over the moon that this opportunity was in front of us.

I tell you this to make my tendency to forget God's goodness to me obvious. Here I was, feeling great about where God had our family, and all it took was my super-patient husband coming home sick to send me into a pity party yet again. You see, that's what I do. I sway from trusting God's loving-kindness and struggling to see His faithfulness on an almost daily basis. My poor husband did not exactly get a sweet, nurturing wife that time around either. Oh, dear reader, if you do not know me well enough to know that while I strive to submit to Hugh and be the Proverbs 31 wife I so desperately desire to be, I am quite far from that most days. I apologize for that harsh revelation. Books don't tend to include videos of my snappy, nagging, "Wash your hands!" or "Hugh, don't cough on the babies!" (The man is not only an adult, he is a doctor. He's kind of aware of these things). While I did feel sorry for him that he wasn't feeling well, a bigger part of me, the sinful part of me, was more concerned with my own fears of the girls getting sick again or me just simply needing a break for a couple hours. So there I was, already forgetting God's goodness to me, already getting stuck on myself rather than looking to the needs of others, and throwing a flat-out pity party. Then the mailman came, and as I looked in the mailbox, hot tears flowed down my face. In the mail were letters from many, many friends from different season of life, bringing encouragement and affirmation. Some of them included little "happies" as well, all of them fond memories or conversations. As I read them, I cried. I cried because of the kindness of the support system in my life; I wept because I needed it so very badly on this very day. What a representation of the grace we have in Christ. Friends, God shows up. He shows up even when we are too consumed with ourselves to grasp the bigger plan. He shows up even when we are throwing a "woe is me" tantrum. We are offered His grace even in the moments we blatantly aren't aware of it, even in the moments where our track record doesn't deserve it. Especially then. Romans 5:8 says it this way: "But God demonstrates His own love for us in this: while we were still sinners, Christ died for us."

I don't deserve this love even on my very best days, but He chooses to lavish it on me because His love has nothing to do with me and everything to do with Him. I am sure that someone correlated that tangible love I received, and for that, I am unbelievably thankful. Here's where coincidence or human love just doesn't explain it: along with those letters, there was a package from a friend who I had helped walked through the adoption process before the girls were born. I expected to receive a couple of shirts that I had ordered from her in support of another friend's adoption, but she had included an extra handful of shirts, a beautiful bracelet, and a precious letter. Friends, these things do not happen by accident. God times things perfectly and loves on us through those around us, and I believe He is up in heaven, giddily thinking about all the gifts He has yet to bestow on us. I cannot wait until we get to heaven and get to sit around and talk through all the things that He planned, and all the intricate details involved, including the ones that we did not catch or notice. He shows up always.

That night, as I cared for my sick husband, while there was some anxiety still present over what the upcoming week would hold, I also had a different perspective that was brought through the hands, feet, and heart of Christ through His children. I was reminded that He is faithful and loving in all things, and that this love surpasses all unexpected, expected, happy moments, and trials to come. While not every day brings us reminders of this through letters and gifts from friends, my prayer for you today is that you would be made aware of His love that is all around you as the life He has breathed into you continues to unfold. He is working, friends, and He is constantly making His love know to us. I was so very thankful for the lessons He had taught me through our loving support system, and I was ready to move forward with whatever He had in mind.

Lessons Learned

* In what area of your life do you most struggle with having a performance mind-set? Is it difficult for you to believe you serve an audience of one? Why or why not?
* When do you find it hardest to see God's goodness toward you or toward those around you?
* Through who, what, where, or when has God showed up when you needed it most? How has He reminded you of His love for you through the community around you?

CHAPTER 19

HIS BEST

‿⟋

July 2014

*"I thank You, Lord, that You were too wise to heed my feeble prayers
and answer as I sought, since these rich gifts Your bounty has bestowed
have brought me more than all I asked or thought; Giver of good, so
answer each request with Your own giving, better than my best."*

—ANNIE JOHNSON FLINT

THERE WAS SOMETHING THAT PAINED my heart to the core during that
season of waiting, something I was not able to verbalize until one weekend
in July when a light bulb went off. I was getting weary of comments, both
from myself and others, that implied we were waiting on our girls to "get
better," as if whatever was going on with them was some kind of illness.
It wasn't. There were moments where I felt like so much of our life, both
personal and in the various therapies the girls attended, was focused on
their performance. I was as guilty as the next, but that humid July morning, I recognized that as a mind-set that had become exhausting. There
is probably a question in the back of your minds, a question that those
closest to me dared to ask, and I would like to address it: "Morgan, if you
could wake up tomorrow morning and all the girls' struggles could be
gone, would you choose that?" This was something I spent many days

pondering. In my finite human mind, I will always have the tendency to choose the comfortable and to latch on to what the world considers normal. However, as I looked back on those fourteen months and thought of all that God had done, both in my heart and the hearts of those around us, my soul could not proclaim that I would change a bit of it. Watching God get glory is addictive, and I was slowly learning that whatever He placed in our hands was absolutely best. There was a time in my life where I might have said that I believed this, but it wasn't stuck to the core of who I was. Praise God, for He was giving me the grace to have eyes to see through His lenses and very truthfully, I had become comfortable with our story as His plan A. This is a truth I want us to explore.

I have found so much solace in the book *Streams in the Desert* by L. B. Cowman. It has helped me to change my perspective on suffering altogether. One of my favorite quotes from it is as follows: "Faith does not say, 'I see this is good for me, therefore God must have sent it.' Instead, faith declares, 'God sent it, therefore it must be good for me.'"

What a backward attitude from that which we tend to think! So often, our pride gets in the way, and we begin to think that we are sacrificing by letting God place something bad in our lives. We sing worship songs at the top of our lungs, belting out lines about surrender but forgetting that the true focus is Him. I was unbelievably guilty of this during the first year and a half of the girls' lives. It was as if I was saying to God, "You should be super impressed with me for not throwing a fit about this horrible thing you have brought upon us." Friends, don't we believe that if He has brought it upon us, it is truly His best? Don't we believe that the Word promises us that He works all things together for good and that simultaneously, His ways are not our own? (Romans 8:28; Isaiah 55:8). I am not at all suggesting that it is not tough, living on this side of heaven in our flesh, to comprehend some of the things He brings. It is so easy for me to think the grass is greener on the other side. I was quick to fall into the trap of wondering why some people seemed to be able to gallop through this life with comforts abounding and often lusted after what having children who were developing typically would look like.

In the first year of life, the girls went to the doctor more times than most adults ever go. We spent our days and moments in therapy, while many people frolicked from play date to play date. Oh, for my biggest worry to have been what discipline would look like in our family. Here's some true honesty: I even sometimes went to a place where I believed we were being allowed the suffering because we had some level of closeness with the Lord that the comfortable people did not. Ugh, the grossness of my sin! This actually couldn't be further from the truth. What is best for me is not going to be best for you. That's why God is God, and I am not. Yes, there are absolute commands and promises in His word that are given to us all, but we must never fall into the trap of thinking that the temporary things of this world are included in this. It can be played out in so many ways in all of our lives.

Think about the setup of a high school basketball game. I remember that, more often than not (outside of parents and friends), most people would show up right before the varsity team began to play. The junior varsity team was somewhat of an appetizer for what was to come. Friends, whatever God's plan is for your life, let's stop treating it like we are at the JV game. This is God's best for your life today. And if tomorrow, your circumstances change, those will now be His new best for your life. We have to stop looking for our tomorrows as a source of satisfaction. I will not speak on Joel Osteen, as I have never met the man and have never read any of his books, but I can speak on the title of one of them, *God's Best for Your Life: Seven Steps to Living at Your Full Potential*. I am here to say that the Bible clearly lets you know there are not seven magical steps. No. There is simply one: Jesus. Putting your hope and faith in His righteousness, His provision, and His love are truly the only way to be at peace in this fallen world that we in. I do not know what is going on in your life, but whatever it is, I know that it is not plan B. There is nothing that is going to happen tomorrow that is going to bring any more fulfillment than what He has for you today, albeit Himself. He is enough. We must refuse to live with an attitude of, "I will make the best of today knowing that when x, y, or z arrives or changes, things will be better." No. The reality of it is this: no relationship, no job, no title, no amount of money, no weight loss, nothing material, no child, no change in health status, *nothing* is going to bring you any more eternal joy than what is already being offered to you today in Jesus. This was true with our family as well. The girls were not on the B team, and this wasn't God's way of making the best out of a subpar situation; this *was* His best for them, for Hugh and myself, for our entire family, for our friends, for God's kingdom, and for the world. Ally and Bailey Grace were perfect just the way they were. Seriously. This was not a cop-out; this is the truth laid out for you in God's word. They both were fearfully and wonderfully made in His image, exactly how He wanted them to be. We rejoice in that both then and now. Their unique qualities were not burdens; they were blessings that allowed us to see more of the Lord is each and every day. We will always be indebted to Him and to you for being instruments in His all-wise, all-knowing hands.

Regardless, I was fighting to believe these truths on that particular day, allowing the emotions within me to suggest otherwise and tempt me to look into my neighbor's yard and wonder what it would be like to live under their terms. I fought to praise Him for all that was, not all that I wished could be because the reality of who He is frees us to live joyfully in the present moment without questioning why and without wondering if there is something else out there that we are missing out on. This is my prayer for you today as well, dear reader: that you would be able to look at your current circumstance with gratitude and contentment, knowing that His plans for you are good. He is working a beautiful tapestry of Himself in all things; and I had begun to fight to believe that truth more than ever before.

Lessons Learned

* Do you believe God is giving His best to you? Why or why not?
* When have you been most tempted to lust after your neighbor's life instead of being content with your own? Explain.
* Do you believe that everything you need for satisfaction is available to you today? How can we encourage one another to believe this more fully in our day-to-day lives?

CHAPTER 20

EVEN NOW

$\smile$

July 2014

"For it is You who light my lamp; the Lord
my God lightens my darkness."

—PSALM 18:28

IT WAS AT ANOTHER ONE of many doctor's appointments that I noticed her. She was sitting next to us in the waiting room, and I guessed her daughter to be about fourteen years old, but much younger in mind. The girl was holding a raggedy stuffed animal, and she was not speaking a word. She stared straight ahead, without much interaction with the world around her. Her mother sat next to her, and years of sitting in that very waiting room and the worry that ensued had her looking much older than I am sure she was. I had to ask. I spoke with her mom for a minute about which doctors they saw (too many to count), and then gently asked her what her daughter's diagnosis was. "We have just named it after her at this point. No diagnosis after fourteen years of looking," she coarsely replied. Fourteen years without a diagnosis. The girl's name was called, and the mom led her daughter to whichever appointment she needed to go. All I could feel was anger—angry for their family for having to live with such an obvious disease without having a prognosis or name and angry for myself at the thought of being thirteen years down this road and knowing nothing. Angry.

At points in this journey, I tended to write from a place in which I let you in on the lesson learned after the wrestling occured, but in those moments, I wrote from a place in which I was still in the battle. My God was always victorious in it; this I know. That week found me in a familiar place of weariness, as we continued to find ourselves in the in-between. I was jealous, envious of those who seemed to have answers about their children.

So here we sat, at a doctor's appointment I had been praying about for months. I looked forward to it in the sense that I really felt like this physician was going to be able to lead us closer to some answers. I left the appointment feeling defeated, insecure, and beat down. After some time of discussing and examining our girls, he told me I needed to stop living for a diagnosis because he believed there was a good chance we would not find one. This man, who knows nothing about me or who I am desperately trying to live for, namely Christ, reminded me that God is greater than a diagnosis. In that moment, however, it wasn't enough. I locked myself in an isolated place for the next few days. This is a place where the enemy loved to keep me, one in which I determined that no one understands therefore no one could encourage. As I tried to reason with this man on why a diagnosis was important, he said words that still sting my heart when I replay them: "Mrs. Cheek, if your girls were to die in ten years, they would die with or without a diagnosis." At that point, I shut down altogether and just walked through the rest of the appointment numb. It was a meeting, which I had counted as a gift, that was beginning to feel like a knife to my very heart—angry.

I thought back to the woman in the waiting room, and while our girls' mystery is much different than hers, I placed myself in her shoes. "God," I whispered in the car, "I don't think I could do it. I can't wait that long. It's too much." Doubt.

When I had days where the edges of our story cut too deep, I tended to check out emotionally in order to survive and take care of the girls in the way that they deserved. I would spend a day or so going through the motions and lifting up feeble prayers that God would enter back into the story and help me, forgetting that He was holding the pen and writing it all Himself.

Music and the outdoors have always served as therapy for me and remind me how small I am in the midst of a bigger story. As I walked outside the day after this appointment, trying to praise God in the hard, a song came on that resonated within my soul. Will Reagan sings, "Even Now," and one of the lines stood out to me the most: "Even now, here's my heart, Lord." Faith. It occurred to me that this was what I was missing altogether. I had prayed for faith for so many years, and here, in the in-between, this was where my faith was being grown and stretched the most. Friends, it is crucial that we proclaim faith in God and His plan at all times. It might be even more important in those in-betweens of life where you feel most suspicious of God's goodness or most betrayed by His plans. After all, isn't that what faith truly is—having eyes to see His presence and purpose at all times and in all things? When we pray that God would enlarge our faith, we cannot be surprised when He does so through not allowing us to see. Faith without sight. Time and time again, the Word reminds us what this looks like. Through the stories of those who have gone before us, we see that faith has been the answer all along. Hebrews 11 is full of examples of people who did the hard thing without having concrete evidence that God would do that which He promised. Faith. Some of them did not even get to see the end results while they were still on earth. Faith. 2 Corinthians 5:7 tells us that, "We walk by faith, not by sight." As I spent time walking through the hard, I found the Lord calling me to say, over and over again, "God, You are greater than a diagnosis. You are greater than a diagnosis. You are greater." Sometimes we have to claim truths we know to be real even when we don't feel them. After all, He is greater than our emotions as well.

I wish I could tell you that after that walk, I was in a place where the peace settled, and I felt joy in our story again. I could not say that, but I could speak this: He who promises is faithful. His faithfulness does not rely on me (2 Timothy 2:13), and He was writing this story. It was going to bring Him glory and us good, no matter what. I was even more committed to praising Him in the gray; even when I didn't necessarily understand it or feel like it. He was always worthy, this I knew. Where are you today? If He is calling you to let your faith be strengthened, let me encourage you to keep battling. He has already made the victory His. He is fighting for you; you need only be still (Exodus 14:14). It is hard, but it serves an eternal purpose. Even now, here's my heart, Lord.

Lessons Learned

* What battle are you wrestling with God about most today?
* When you don't find yourself feeling joy, how do you praise God regardless? Can you praise God even when your emotions are weary? If yes, why and how?
* What situations or people refresh your soul the most? If you are feeling particularly weary today, how can you practically arrange your schedule to make more time for those people or things more in order to nourish your soul this week? If in a group, think about who could serve who in a way that helps foster this.

CHAPTER 21

COMFORTABLE

July 2014

*"Radical obedience to Christ is not easy...it's not comfort, not health,
not wealth, and not prosperity in this world. Radical obedience to
Christ risks losing all these things. But in the end, such risk finds
its reward in Christ. And He is more than enough for us."*

—David Platt

After the hospital visits and the gloomy doctor's appointment, we all needed a break. We decided to head to my parent's cabin in Tennessee, and it was the first time in a while I had felt carefree. There were no therapy visits or doctors to see and no looming news at our front door. It was wonderful.

As I sat on the front porch, sipping on coffee and listening to the bird's chirp, I became aware of the fact that I was not feeling as in tune with the Lord as usual. I could not quite figure out why, and I started trying to think of any unrepentant sin that I was not laying at the cross. Then it hit me. It wasn't that I had set anything between the Lord and myself necessarily; it was that I was feeling comfortable. I cringed at the thought, but I knew it was true. *What's so wrong with being comfortable?* you might be thinking. You see, I would love to be someone who feels like they are equally as close to the Lord in easy and hard times. I would love to be able to state confidently that when things are going great from a worldly perspective, my eyes naturally and immediately stay fixed on the Lord and the things of heaven. But, if I'm honest, I know this isn't true. If I am honest, it is when I am stretched, when I am most uncomfortable, that I am most aware of God's presence. I cannot speak for everyone, but as I look back on my life, I see proof of this in every season. That had been the thing about this journey with our girls that was so refreshing. I was closer to my Savior than ever before. I had been walking through the hardest days of my life, yet I felt a tangible peace in the depths of who I was.

There were some moments from the previous week that I was not proud of in the least. I confessed to the Lord that I was beginning to get scared to continue to glorify His name in our family's life. When I had first chosen to be obedient to share this story, I had a moment with God in which I said, "This is Your story played out in our lives. You do as You choose, and I will continue to give You glory in it all." I don't think I realized the challenges that would come in that. To be truthful, between the hospital visits and the doctor appointments, a part of me had begun to doubt if sharing it all with the world was the best thing. It seemed as if we had been stretched a touch more than I felt comfortable with, and I was almost over being a puppet in it all. Then I remembered Job.

In the book of Job, we see God allow Satan to test Job by stripping him of almost all that he held dear. Job began the book assuring and exhorting his friends that it was out of God's goodness that He had allowed these things to happen, but as the book goes on, Job's desire to know why God allowed the suffering began to overtake His trust in God and His ultimate plan. After Job and his friends blabbered on about this for a while, God stepped in and basically went through the crux of all creation. He reminded Job that since Job was not there from the beginning of time, he surely could not question the Creator's choices and decisions for His own children. The thing is, Job had forgotten that the play, this kingdom, was not based on Job but on God Himself. Oh, how I can relate. When I think about what we are walking through now, if I'm not careful, I can begin to question the "whys" in light of us being at the center of the story. The problem with that is that we are not. Friends, I realize that can be a hard truth to swallow, but I want to remind us that whenever we are so consumed with our circumstances and our own stuff, and we begin to think we deserve differently, we are in the wrong. How do we know what we deserve? As a Christian, I say that I believe the wages of sin are death and that I therefore deserve death outside of the grace of Jesus Christ. That being said, if we are in the business of thinking we "deserve" differently, we are right. I don't want to get what I deserve! We have been spared more than we could ever be worthy of because of God's mercy through Christ, and I never want to live in light of anything else.

Back to being comfortable. That summer weekend, it wasn't that I was doing anything wrong. But when I find myself comfortable, I tend to find myself running out the door on God, occasionally thanking Him for a relaxing time but pretty much checking out altogether. This is not sinful necessarily, but it pains me to think of how easily I can fix my eyes on the seen rather than the unseen. Romans 8 reminds us that peace comes from setting our minds on the things of the Spirit rather than the things of the flesh. Why? Because the things of the Spirit are eternal. As I often point out to my own heart and yours, a fun weekend fades. Looking forward to things as a gift from God is not wrong, but if we are looking forward to something in order to be satisfied, we are going to be left wanting each and every time. My friend, Liz, once told me that she was envious of Hugh and I and what we are walking through with the girls. She went on to say that she felt like we had something that constantly puts us at the Lord's feet, and I could not agree more. In a weird way, I knew that this suffering was a privilege. My flesh did not feel that way at all; it was uncomfortable. Truthfully our physical beings will always be uneasy with viewing things in light of heaven. Until we are transformed, we will always be risk of living in light of this temporary world instead of living in light of the freedom offered through Christ. I use to think that there would be some level of spiritual maturity I would reach that would cause me to not desire the things of this world ever again. The problem with that is I absolutely used it as an excuse to sin. *Well,* I would think, *if I still desire these things, I guess I can't help it. Isn't it up to God to make me not want these things anymore?* Yes and no. Yes, it is absolutely God working in you in order to sanctify you; as you know Him more, your desires most definitely change. What isn't biblical is thinking that the flesh is just altogether not there once you become a believer. There is a huge difference in salvation and sanctification. We were saved at the cross once and for all, and as soon as we accept that in faith, we are saved. Sanctification is a process that happens over time, and it will continue to be played out until Jesus chooses to bring us to Himself face-to-face. I believe God chooses to make us uncomfortable in our flesh in order to make us more comfortable in Him. *Sanctification.* I also believe that it is a beautiful paradox to know that we are dust but to also know that we are wholly, fully, unconditionally loved dust made in the image of God. We must be careful to not view one side without knowledge of the other.

So how do we live in the midst of the comfortable? How do we choose to accept both comfort and discomfort as blessings, while not desiring anything but the lot the Lord has chosen for us? The truth is, not everyone is called to suffer at all times. Sure, there is a level of suffering that exists simply because we live in a broken world, but we are not all called to really hard seasons at all times. After all, if we were all hurting deeply, who would serve as the hands and feet of Christ? Who would be there to support the members of the body that desperately need the comfort of others around them? When we are feeling comfortable on this side of heaven, we must never give them the glory that the Giver Himself deserves. We must accept all things as good, and pray for His eyes in each of our moments. That way, when we are faced with trial and tribulation, we do not have to be surprised or in despair because we have already been living with our hands wide open, ready to accept whatever comes our way.

After being at the river for the weekend, back to the normal grind that included doctor and therapy appointments and the reality of my own two hands being in charge of two babies, I smiled and my heart felt at peace. You see, I was learning to embrace the uncomfortable. Instead of shaking my fists at heaven or trying to change our reality, I was learning to praise

God in the midst of it. He was my comfortable. He was my peace. He was why, in the middle of a season of unknowns and consuming disabilities, I was able to stand strong. His strength was my weakness—only Him. Whether you feel at home with what you are walking through or you are being stretched to the max, I want to encourage you to stop searching for something different. Whatever your lot, allow Him to change your perspective to viewing it all in light of His kingdom, not the one you wish existed. His way is best. I didn't want to look to petty comforts to satisfy me; I wanted to look to Him. May this be said of each of us, today.

Lessons Learned

* Do you find yourself feeling closer to God when you are comfortable or uncomfortable in your current situation? Why do you think this is?
* In what season of life did you feel closest to God? Why?
* How do you think we choose to accept both comfort and discomfort as blessings? Give examples of those around you who have done this well.

CHAPTER 22

GRACE

August 2014

"Never yield to gloomy anticipation. Place your hope and confidence in God. He has no record of failure."

—Mrs. Charles L. Cowman

"When my anxious thoughts multiply within me, Your consolations delight my soul."

—Psalm 94:19

THERE WAS A TIME IN my life where I talked myself into being a runner. I actually ran a half marathon and began training for a full marathon in college with a friend who legitimately enjoys running. (This always boggles my mind that those people really exist). We ran nineteen miles one day, and I was miserable for two days after. I woke up one morning, had a come-to-Jesus moment where I admitted to myself that I hated running, and I don't think I have run more than a couple miles at a time ever since. I never ran the full marathon (sorry, Cassie!).

The first week of August, I decided I was going to go on a run to try and sort through some things. Do you ever just have those weeks where you wake up on the wrong side of the bed every single day? I go through days, sometimes a week at a time, where I rise in a funk and can't seem to really get out of it. Different reasons bring it on, but God being God always helps me to do a heart check on why. The thing is that there is always a reason. Often during these days, I find myself fighting being just plain short, sometimes mean, to those I am closest with whenever I feel this way. I hate this about myself. As Paul says in Romans, however, "I do not understand what I do. For what I want to do I do not do, but what I hate I do" (7:15).

Anyone relate? Anyone have those moments that if they were videotaped and shown to those on the outside, you would cringe?

I may or may not have the song "Despicable Me" by Pharrell Williams, from the Disney movie, on a playlist I have. Since I was attempting to run (let's call it more of a jog), I happily left it playing when it came on. And then, it hit me. Here are the words from the beginning: "I'm havin' a bad, bad day. It's about time that I get my way, steam rollin' whatever I see. Huh, despicable me. I'm havin' a bad, bad day. If you take it personal, that's OK. Watch, this is so fun to see. Huh, despicable me."

It goes on and the lead of the song keeps asking "why?" about everything. One negative thought about having a bad day changed his thoughts on his whole day altogether. Sound familiar? It sure does to me.

Honesty time: I was over it. I was over being stretched to the limit in every area of my family's life, so it seemed. This new season had challenged our faith, our marriage, our family relationships, our friendships, our finances, and our expectations and plans as a whole. I told Hugh that morning that I was ready to have a break in just one area of our lives. This feeling of being "over it" had slipped in to my interactions with those around me, often through the seemingly small negative thoughts that I allowed to pass in my mind. I had told God how "over it" I was, and it seemed He had responded in silence. He had not given us anymore of an idea of prognosis or expectations for the girls, had pushed us even more financially, and our expectations still stood in the gap, wanting. Those were

His choices, but I began to realize that the way I handled His choices was up to me. What I choose to do with His plans for my life, how I choose to react, is up to me. Every day, we wake up with a choice. We can choose to trust God, to allow Him to reign and rule, and to let His Spirit control our thoughts and our interactions or we can give into the mind-set that says, "It's about time that I get my way." Let's think about that for a moment. Is it about time for you to get your way? Is it? I believe if we took a strong look at the grace around us, we would be filled with gratitude instead of frustration of the glory around us. So this is what I attempted to do on my run.

Back to the run. The entire time I was jogging, there were birds in the field. I probably saw one hundred robins, all trusting that the Lord was going to provide, just as He always had. They were not looking around to the other birds, afraid that their food was being taken; they trusted that there was enough for all—limitless provision and limitless grace. As the Word says, "Look at the birds of the air; they neither sow nor reap nor gather into barns, and yet your heavenly Father feeds them. Are you not of more value than they?" (Matthew 6:26).

Well...aren't you? The birds are not complaining about the fact they have to eat worms all day; they are just thankful He has brought them their fill.

"You open Your hand and satisfy the desires of every living thing."
—Psalm 145:16

Not one promise of the Lord's has returned void. If we are not aware of His provisions, it is not because He is not giving; it is because we are too worried about getting what we think we need and not trusting His gifts.

Not two minutes after this revelation did I begin thinking about how gloomy of a day it was—negative thinking. It was a pattern that had so infiltrated my thoughts that I sometimes didn't even recognize how much it was affecting my spirit or rather His Spirit's ability to live through me.

"Do not conform to the pattern of this world, but be transformed by the renewing of your mind. Then you will be able to test and approve what God's will is—His good, pleasing, and perfect will."
—Romans 12:2

This world is full of excuses to make ourselves the focus. "Me, me, me," is the cry of all that is around us. Magazines and media all seem to say, "What are *you* getting out of this?" God's word completely opposes this, telling us that we should forget about self all together and that we should pick up Christ's cross and trust the lot He has given us. The truth is that the quickest way to misery is to make the focus of our life on what we are getting out of it. In marriage, the moments I spend keeping count of who is getting more or giving more are the moments I am the most annoying to live with and the most discontent. The times where I choose to love Hugh with a love outside of myself, namely Christ, and not worry about what I'm getting in return are the times that I am the most full of joy. Counterculture? Yes. Biblical and true? Absolutely.

We must constantly keep ourselves in check with what we allow to dwell in our minds. What we think matters, and we must never believe the lie that thoughts are less real than action. The heart behind them is the same. Matthew 5:28 says, "But I tell you that anyone who looks at a woman lustfully has already committed adultery with her in his heart." What we think matters. We must fight the tendency to let our minds just wonder aimlessly. Our flesh's desire is always going to head toward the things of this world rather than the things of God. We must make the choice to allow God to take over the very passing of thoughts in our minds. If that sounds intense to you, or impossible, I want to gently remind you that it is through the Spirit of God that we have the ability to do any and all things He puts us up to; furthermore, Scripture makes it clear that what we store up treasure in is where our heart will be also (Matthew 6:21). Even when my emotions don't connect with it, how I desire my treasure to be in the eternal things and not my temporary frustrations. This starts in the mind. So in the midst of my casual thoughts about the gloominess of that day, the Lord had me catch a few glimpses of blue in the sky. Yes, I had to look closely to see it, but, my lack of being aware of it at first glance didn't make it any less there. Suddenly I saw a beautiful bluebird in the midst of all the robins. I began thinking about all the things in our life that are not challenging. The fact that Hugh and I both woke up healthy that morning. That our girls were no longer ill. That I could take in deep breaths. That the clouds in the sky were actually causing the heat to be less intense. That we have an amazing church family. Food on the table. Shelter. That Hugh has a job that pays the bills. That we even had the opportunity to attempt to find a diagnosis. That our girls were going to be able to be a part of an education system that will have special classrooms for them. That I was able to run. Never mind the things I felt I lacked. I was rich. Beyond that, I had been given true riches: "And my God will meet all your needs according to the riches of His glory in Christ Jesus" (Philippians 4:19).

My true needs go far beyond material things or even temporal health. Our true needs were met once and for all at the cross, and Christ has given us the riches of heaven, limitless for each of our days. It began to rain, and between the raindrops, I marveled at how wonderful it felt—perspective.

Friends, I don't know if this is all foreign to you. I don't know if you wake up joyful each and every day and if all the relationships in your life are free and easy. For some reason, I highly doubt this is true for anyone. I believe that because we live on this side of heaven, challenges abound within and around. This weekend, however, the choice is yours. If you are in Christ, you have the choice to let Him live out all your days and to focus on the beautiful around rather than the seemingly negative, albeit temporary, things that cross your mind. He has promised that He is making all things new and "for from Him and through Him and for Him are all things. To Him be the glory forever! Amen" (Romans 11:36).

I decided I would probably not run again anytime soon, but I was so thankful for the lessons He chose to teach me in those moments. Despicable me, yes. Without Christ, I am rotten through and through. But God, in His wisdom, took these rags and made me new, and He will continue to build His beautiful tapestry that I am eternally grateful to be sewn into. No matter what, that is always something to celebrate. He has eternally provided that which we truly so desperately needed and the only thing that really matters. He is always with us, dear friends. Yesterday, today, and tomorrow, abound with His riches.

Lessons Learned

* Does the phrase "over it" ring a bell with you today? If so, what do you feel "over"?
* Read Romans 12:2 again. Where do you struggle with conforming to the patterns of this world the most? How do you combat it, and what are some was that you could fight against it more?
* Begin praising and thanking God for all the ways He has provided for you today. This week. This month. This year. Beyond. If you are with a group, spend some time thanking Him aloud for His provision in all things.

CHAPTER 23

GROANS OF CREATION

⌒

August 2014

"Earth's best does not compare with heaven's least."

—F. B. MEYER

THE MUNDANE OF OUR NEW normal was becoming a bit smothering, and our family beach trip could not have come at a better time. I love the beach. There is nothing better to me than sitting in the sand, Bible in hand, heart wide open, looking at the beauty around me and contemplating my smallness in light of His big, gorgeous world. I find myself being drawn to the psalms in these moments, and it seems easy for me to say along with David, "From the rising of the sun to its setting, the name of the Lord is to be praised!" (Psalm 113:3). I had not been near the ocean since we had known that there was something going on with our girls, and as I breathed in His goodness around me the first morning, I couldn't help but also contemplate the mysteries of His creation. It's interesting how much I enjoy relaxing by the ocean because as far as the waves go, I have never been a fan. Of course, I love looking at them and hearing their glories as they are preached to all within reach, but I am somewhat afraid of going out in them. It isn't what is underneath (I grew in jumping into the muddy, far from clear waters of the Hiwassee River, and had no problem touching ankles with a fish or two). What scares me is the unpredictable tossing to and fro of the waves themselves and the lack of control I have with the size of the wave that hits me. And here I was, being thrown into an ocean of His mysteries in our life, not having any say in whether I wanted a wave as tall and mysterious as the one I was now swimming in.

Of all the things I am grateful for in this life, my family is at the very top of the list. This beach trip was a perfect depiction of how they handled this new season of our little family's life. They did not treat the girls' condition like an elephant in the room, but they also did not make it any sort of focus. They did not talk about ways that they saw the girls "getting better;" they just loved them where they were without reservation. They were also well aware that while it has been challenging for everyone involved, no one hurt or struggled more deeply than Hugh and myself. They did not ask us any medical questions unless we brought them up ourselves, which, in ways that were unbelievably refreshing, Hugh and I have chose not to do much on that trip. It was not that we wanted to deny a second of it, nor was it that it wasn't on our minds at almost every waking moment. It's just that sometimes it was nice to just live life with people and rejoice in the here and now. Scratch that—it is always nice to just live life with people and rejoice in the here and now. Tomorrow has enough trouble of its own.

My sister and I sat on the beach one of the last days of the trip, waves crashing around and within me, and I tore through a layer of my heart that I didn't tend to get near—the anger and bitterness that crept up in the midst of our somewhat unusual circumstances. I believe and celebrate God's sovereignty, authority, and overall goodness in all of our lives. Hand in hand with that, I grieved and hurt in ways that took my breath away if I thought about them too much. As tears stung my eyes, my sister patiently and sympathetically waited as I tried to flesh these gut-wrenching feelings out. The truth was, I didn't know how to process the fact that I trusted God and mourned reality all at the same time. How can you explain the paradox of knowing that if you could do it all over, you wouldn't change something in light of the glory God has been given, while also knowing good and well if you had a magic wand today and your flesh was weak, you might bail out? It's hard. It's messy. It's God's plan for humanity wrapped up in our small piece of the puzzle.

> For I consider that the sufferings of this present time are not worth comparing with the glory that is to be revealed to us. For the creation waits with eager longing for the revealing of the sons of God. For the creation was subjected to futility, not willingly, but because of Him who subjected it, in hope that the creation itself will be set free from its bondage to corruption and obtain the freedom of the glory of the children of God. For we know that the whole creation has been groaning together in the pains of childbirth until now. And not only the creation, but we ourselves, who have the first fruits of the Spirit, groan inwardly as we wait eagerly for adoption as sons, the redemption of our bodies. For in this hope we were saved. Now hope that is seen is not hope. For who hopes for what he sees? But if we hope for what we do not see, we wait for it with patience.
> —Romans 8:18–24

Ann Voskamp, in her book *One Thousand Gifts*, talks about a moment she had with her brother-in-law when he was about to lose another child (his second) to the same genetic disease that killed his first. She says it this way:

> "If it were up to me..." and then the words pound, desperate and hard, "I'd write this story differently." I regret the words as soon as they leave me. They seem so un-Christian, so unaccepting—so, No, God! I wish I could take them back, comb out their tangled madness, dress them in their calm Sunday best. But there they are, released and naked, raw and real, stripped of any theological cliché, my exposed, serrated howl to the throne room."

There they were. The same words I had uttered to God in moments of weakness, exposed in Ann's writing and already written on my heart. As I thought about them that morning, I was brought to the preceding verses in Romans, and my soul felt relieved and understood yet again. Paul said it himself! The Lord knows that we would not have been subjected to suffering willingly. That's why, in His wisdom, He suffered for us. We love because He first loved us (1 John 4:19), and just because we were choosing to trust Him and accept His plans for us, didn'tt mean we weren't stumbling through it in our flesh. My soul cried out, "Yes!" to God while my flesh writhed in the frustration.

I saw little pieces of the anger and bitterness in my interaction with others, sometimes more often in those I loved most. At times, it was subtle and not noticeable. Other times, it appeared blatantly. I shamefully talked to my sister about this, telling her how I hated it but felt like it was inevitable at times, and she freed me up to give myself grace in the midst of my humanity. There was pride and fear in the fact that I didn't want to go there. The prideful part of me wanted sin to be dead and gone in it all and was ashamed that I couldn't seem to be sanctified in all things at all times. The fearful part of me was afraid that if I stared some of the hard emotions in the eye, I would be consumed by them and unable to see truth. Here's the reality: until we who believe meet Jesus face-to-face, there are going to be bits of sin mixed in with loads of His limitless grace. That's the thing about Jesus: He is most aware of the continued rebellion of our hearts, but His love compels Him to toss it as far as the east is from the west. So goes the cross. He died so that we could day to day choose to live for Him. He was slain on the cross so that in moments when we feel slain, we can look to Him and see it nailed and finished. It is a glorious paradox—suffering and brokenness around and within, but righteousness constantly making all these new. Beyond that, because of this love, we are not consumed. Nothing can separate us from Him, not even ourselves and our own messiness.

The vacation would be over in a few days, and it would be time to go back to the day-to-day routine. The upcoming week had pieces in it that took my breath away and hards that I would like to pretend were not coming. We had an appointment scheduled with a world-renowned physician who might be able to give us some beneficial but hard information on the girls, and I had no idea what this appointment would look like. But you know what? In all of it, He would meet me there. In the anger and bitterness. In the happy and easy. In the questions and "what ifs." He meets us in all of our moments.

So where does that leave you? What are the parts of your heart that you wish didn't exist? What are the things that you are afraid of approaching out of fear of where they might lead you? Friends, God's Word promises us that nothing can separate us from Him. Not ourselves. Not the opinions of others. Not those awful emotions we try to keep locked deep inside. All is exposed to Him, and instead of turning away, He looks on us with compassion and asks us to give it to Him. As we do, He takes it, puts it back up at the cross where it belongs, and continues to clothe us in the things that only He can produce in us. He is working in all things, dear reader. All is grace. Let's allow Him to love us in the midst of it all today.

Lessons Learned

- What figurative waves are crashing around or within you today? Are there layers of your heart that you normally do not address with God, yourself, or others? If yes, why?
- Read Romans 8:18–24 again. What stands out to you the most about these verses?
- Where do you find your soul crying out, "Yes," while your flesh writhes in frustration?
- What runs through your mind and heart when you hear the phrase, "Nothing can separate you from His love"? What makes this hardest to believe?

CHAPTER 24

THE JOY WITHIN

August 2014

"But I will hope continually and will praise You yet more and more."

—Psalm 71:4

WE CAME HOME FROM A vacation week full of sunshine, delicious food, family, friends, and relaxation. There were extra hands and help all around me, and lots of time to slip away to the beach and spend time alone with my Savior. I found myself back to the day to day- dishwasher emptied, Bible opened in hands, getting ready to get the girls fed and ready for physical therapy, the noises in the background being less ocean, more neighborhood Monday scuffling.

Halfway across the world, the unthinkable occured. Men, women, and children were being tortured, raped, and killed out of the depths of evil of the human heart. The magnitude of it, the genocide, was unimaginable. Toss your child off the mountain so they do not have to walk through such horror. A quick death is better than an ending full of such horrendous suffering. I truly could not fathom having to make this choice for myself, much less my child. It is easy to skirt it all under the rug when it isn't in front of our faces. I didn't want to forget that it wasn't all a movie; it was the reality of our fellow human beings.

There is an unbelievable amount of suffering that occurs on a daily basis. Between the news and our own circle of family and friends, each of us has tragedy placed all around us. So much brokenness and hurting right in our own homes. How do we find joy in light of it all? How do we spend time laughing with those we love on vacation when brokenness abounds? We can't ignore it. We can't shut our eyes to it all. So what do we do? Does God call us to happiness on this side of heaven or mere existence?

This was something I contemplated often during those months of waiting. To many of you, this concept of joy in suffering is extremely foreign. To some, our family's story may be "too much" in the sense that my emotions and hurts are displayed sentence after sentence. There is a culture in our world that wants to encourage us to pacify our pain with the temporary things around us. Had a hard day? Get some ice cream or a glass of wine. Tired on a Monday morning? Drink a little extra coffee. Feeling sad? Find a pill to take the sorrow away. Need to feel wanted? Give yourself to anyone and everyone around you. Whatever you do, do anything to not process or focus on the reality of the hard around and within you. I could be as guilty as the next at wanting to run away from suffering and hold on to the easy and to jump from one exciting thing on the calendar to the next. Here's the problem: it doesn't take away the hard; this behavior just ignores it. It doesn't take much looking back on history to see that while some things have changed, some things have remained the same. Suffering has existed from the moment that Eve took that first bite of the fruit. From that moment on, sin rooted its ugly head in all our lives, and while we can pretend it isn't there, it doesn't change its reality.

Right after our beach trip, someone asked me if I was happy. I tried to find the words to attempt to explain where I was at with happiness but could not seem to do so. The truth was that I was somewhat over the word "happy." To me, happy expressed an emotion void of all hurts. A smile on your face at all times. Carefree living. This, I was definitely not, but what I had was joy. In fact, I believe that in light of the suffering God had allowed in our lives, I experienced more joy than I ever had before.

A few years prior, I would have placed a good bit of hope in a fun week at the beach. I would have built it up in my head, and when it was over, I would have come home feeling pretty empty. Sure, I would have said that my hope was in God alone, but sometimes it takes affliction to truly bring us to a place where this is truth in our lives. Those days, the reality of our lives did not change. We had twins with special needs, and I was faced with the questions and hardships that go along with this at all times. I knew that, with good intentions, many people thought that "getting a break" from it all could fix things. But the truth was, just because I was not there or on "mommy duty" didn't mean it wasn't still going to be there when I got home. Beyond that, while I enjoyed spending time alone with Hugh or friends, and while time away occasionally is healthy for everyone, the thing I really wanted to portray is that even in the midst of all the pain, I loved being their mommy. I loved mommy duty! Just because pain and hurt was a piece of the puzzle didn't mean that it wasn't joyful. So goes all of our lives on this side of heaven.

Here's the thing: we are all going to experience pain and suffering. We are all going to walk through hard things, some seasons being tougher than others. Those of us who have experienced the unexpected might have a layer of this that never goes away. We do not have to deny the reality of it when our hope goes beyond today. If our hope was in something here on earth, it would be depressing to constantly be aware of the hards. If we didn't have the knowledge that one day, there would be no more tears and no more pain, than the smart thing would be to spend our lives trying to avoid it all. But because of Christ, because of the hope we have in Him, we are never in despair. We have joy in suffering. The truth is this: I found the deeper my suffering was, the stronger my joy was. You see, the joy wasn't based on anything around us. Joy is based on the knowledge of Him, and He and His promises have always been the same and always will be. Walking through that season, God taught me to long for heaven like never before. I longed for Him. I craved the day that He takes away all the brokenness, both in my life and the lives of those around me. And you know what? I don't think I would have really wanted Him to come back if things had gone easy peasy. I think I would have desired to live the comfortable, long life that the American dream falsely promises… and then, would have wanted to meet up with Jesus after it was all over. But now? Now God had opened my eyes to the innumerable amount of pain that so many walk through. I realized the magnitude that He went through on the cross when He took all the sin of the world onto Himself. I wanted to be face-to-face with the One who did this out of love and to finally be able to comprehend what it means to know Him fully. But in light of this, how do we enjoy the here and now and the moments that pass before that day comes? I believe it is through walking each moment always aware that we will one day be with Him that causes us to live fully right now. This is true joy—being able to take each and every second as a gift from God, whatever the moment holds, knowing that He is making all things new. This is where I was in August of 2014. I knew that the reality of our earth was not going anywhere. I also knew that bigger than that, more powerful than that, was a God who had taken it all and nailed it to a cross for all eternity. Someday all of our hurt and all of our pain is going away. These hardships are truly temporary. It's like seeing a movie for the second time and knowing the ending. Instead of grieving the middle, you can relax and smile at what's to come, which is way better than happiness that is based on circumstances and fleeting moments. It is true joy. And you know what? Having this mind-set causes each day to be that much more beautiful. It causes you to seek out the true, never-fading beauty in all people and all things. It helps you to navigate the struggles gracefully, knowing that they truly are passing.

Yes, we had been hit with a truth for our lives that prevented me from viewing this world with all rainbows and giggles, but wow, what training it had given me for all eternity. While I may not wear rose-colored glasses on earth, I had heavenly lenses that carry far more riches than anything more comfortable circumstances could ever offer. When I wrote or spoke about our girls, not a single word was said or typed in anything but pure joy, which was much more satisfying than false hopes of anything this side of heaven had to offer. Don't let the presence of pain overshadow the glory and magnitude of the God behind it all.

Friends, the choice that was ours, then, is yours today. We all have the choice to seek out the happiness that is based on situations and comfort or we can seek out the eternal joy that comes from the knowledge of Him. Every moment can be full of His riches that never fade if we would just have eyes to see. It was not easy then, and I can promise you this: it will always be challenging simply because it is so counter-cultural. It will stretch you beyond your emotions, beyond what you think you desire. But you know what? It will be worth it. He will be worth it. And on that day when He chooses to walk us into His courts, we will be able to bow down before Him, arms open wide, and confidently whisper the same name we have desperately desired to lean on: Jesus. Let's seek true joy, albeit Him, today.

So teach us to number our days, that we may get a heart of wisdom. Return, O Lord! How long? Have pity on your servants! Satisfy us in the morning with your steadfast love, that we may rejoice and be glad all our days. Make us glad for as many days as you have afflicted us, and for as many years as we have seen evil. Let your work be shown to your servants, and your glorious power to their children.
—Psalm 90:12–16

Lessons Learned

* Where have you seen God use suffering and affliction to bring you more joy?
* Do you believe we can rejoice and mourn at the same time? If so, how and why?
* Who or what has caused you to see God in the middle of what the world would see as tragedy? Do you know God more or less because of the trials that He has allowed? Why?
* Do you think God can relate to suffering? Why or why not?

CHAPTER 25

A PIECE OF THE PUZZLE

August 2014

The hill was steep, but cheered along the way by conversation sweet, climbing with the thought that it might be so till the height was reached; but suddenly a narrow winding path appeared, and then the Master said, "My child, here you will walk safest with Me alone. I trembled, yet my heart's deep trust replied, "So be it, Lord." He took my feeble hand in His, accepting thus my will to yield to Him. All, and to find all in Him. One long, dark, moment, and no friend I saw, save Jesus only. But oh! So tenderly He led me on and up, and spoke to me such words of cheer, such secret whisperings of His wondrous love, that soon I told Him all my grief and fear, and leaned on His strong arm confidingly. And then I found my footsteps quickened, and light unspeakable, the rugged way illumined, such light as only can be seen in close companionship with God. A little while, and we will meet again—the loved and lost—but in the rapturous joy of greetings, such as here we cannot know, and happy song, and heavenly embraces, and tender recollections rushing back of life now passed, I think one memory more dear and sacred than the rest, will rise, and we who gather in the golden streets, will oft be stirred to speak with grateful love of that dark day Jesus called us to climb some narrow steep, leaning on Him alone.

—DANIEL CRAWFORD

AUGUST WENT FROM CIRCUMSTANCIALLY HARD to harder. It was challenging emotionally, physically, and more. While we didn't get a specific diagnosis for our girls, we were given a handful of painful news that I was not sure I knew how to swallow. It had been something Hugh and I had feared for a while, so in a sense, it was relieving to be told our worst suspicion. Yet, in spite of our wondering, there are some things in life you cannot be prepared for no matter how much you have thought about it before. The doctors were now saying that whatever was going on with the girls stemmed from their brains. One of my favorite physicians I have met thus far gently explained to me why, anatomically, this was starting to look true. I never talked about the delays outside of gross motor development because frankly, I didn't like thinking about it. For whatever reason, there was something about things being solely muscular that sounded much more appealing. I said to many people in previous months that the hardest thing to face would have been if somehow we found out that there was something going on with the girls' brains, and that week, my fear seemed to be affirmed. What lay ahead was continued waiting, more doctors appointments with new specialists, more MRIs, and more difficulty. I had a few days to begin to process it all, and the Lord started to bring me to a place of gratitude—a place that I realized, no matter what, this was His best for our family, for His kingdom, for Ally and Bailey Grace. That last part stung, and there were still questions I had concerning that truth, but I knew it was just that: truth. In spite of what I felt, He was writing this story and the details came from His merciful pen. His story is always something to be excited about, for I know that He is bringing glory and good out of all things, even the ones that don't make sense to me. On the way to dinner with a friend the night after being given this news, I heard a song that I would normally skim past. The words cut through to my core this time, however, and it felt like the Lord was singing it to my heart, the whole thing. Stephen Curtis Chapman sings, "Glorious Unfolding," and he talks about just that: the glories that God is unfolding in the middle of all this life holds and the way that He is going to bring good from even the hardest moments. Right then and there, I thanked God for all that

He was unfolding in our family, and I truly began to get excited about what's to come, even in light of new challenges. That was until Bailey Grace got sick the next day...followed by Ally...followed by me. There we sat, all three of us fighting fevers, and my attitude went from hopeful to crummy. Bailey Grace's sickness turned to Ally's sickness turned to Hugh and I up in the middle of the night, trying to console two screaming babies. I was mad. I couldn't understand why things had to hit all at once—gut-wrenching news and now more sickness? It didn't seem fair. As I meditated on some verses, this one came to mind: "The thief comes only to steal and kill and destroy. I came that they may have life and have it abundantly" (John 10:10).

Ha. Abundant life? Is this really Your version of abundant life? These are real questions I brought to the Lord. The thing is, when you know what you know—that God is a good God and that you are going to follow Him no matter what—but your current reality is so challenging, you begin to bring these bold questions to Him out of desperation. And this, my friend, is one of the mysteries of our God. He is big. He is worthy. He should never tolerate such questions from a grain of sand like me. Yet, in His love, He gently leads me to the truths I need to remember in these tough moments.

I realized right then and there that it was obvious what the thief was trying to steal: my joy, my faith, and my hope in Christ and His plans for me, meaning that which doesn't fade. The enemy came to kill my spirit and to deaden that within me which God has already made alive...or to at least get me thinking it's dead. He came to destroy our relationships, our families, and our outlook on eternity. But Christ? Christ came to do the opposite. While circumstances and current realities seem to fade and bring brokenness and suffering, He promises to bring true life abundant. This abundance is not reliant on situations or on anything on this earth, however. It relies on God and His unchanging, always-giving, always-trustworthy, never-ending grace. The Bible says, "Greater is He that is in me than he that is in the world" (1 John 4:4). You see, the vastness God offers in Christ far outweighs the suffering we are walking through now. In fact, He promises us that any suffering we are walking through now doesn't even compare to the glory that will be revealed later (Romans 8:18). Furthermore, today, we can have abundance of spirit when we allow Him to reign in our lives. The Word says that, "...those who live according to the flesh set their minds on the things of the flesh, but those who live according to the Spirit set their minds on the things of the Spirit. *For to set the mind on the flesh is death, but to set the mind on the Spirit is life and peace*" (Romans 8:5–6, emphasis mine).

See that last part? This is what I was missing. My mind was focused on the fading, perishing things of the flesh, not the all-knowing, perfect, never-fading things of the Spirit. No matter what, in Christ, we have hope. We know that whatever we are going through on this side of heaven has a purpose for all eternity and that He is working in all things. Many of us have read the verse in Philippians that says that our God will supply all our needs (4:19), but I think we skim past the last part—according to the riches in Christ Jesus. The riches in Christ Jesus are not based on flesh and blood, but on the joys and promises found in heaven. Not material wealth. Not comfort. Not even success. No, the riches we are guaranteed go much, much deeper and are much more reliable. He promises to give us the ability to hear that your children have something wrong with their brain and not crumble, knowing whatever it is comes from His hand. He gives us the strength to walk through each day, unsure of what tomorrow will look like. It goes on and on, but there is *nothing*—no power, no illness, no person, not even death itself—that can separate us from Him (Romans 8:35–38). So I can look whatever is ahead dead on with confidence that He is walking us through it and that it is good, meaning abundant life. There is no one else who can promise us this. Romantic comedies often imply that when you meet your soul mate, he or she will have the ability to protect you and care for you perfectly. I love Hugh with all my heart and am positive that there isn't a better man for me out there, but here's the thing: he can't take away the pain of what is going on with our girls. He cannot love me perfectly in this. Deuteronomy 32:12 says, "The Lord alone led him." In our wilderness, in those moments where the pain goes deeper than any fix this world has to offer, He is our hope. Only He can truly walk us through all the valleys of life while giving us His peace and comfort along the way. Friends, we must fix our eyes on Him alone. Whether you are on a mountain or a valley, He is the only one who can give us the riches that come from His unfading Spirit. All others things will pass away, but He remains. This is where our eyes must be—Him.

My flesh was bruised and hurting, both physically and emotionally. I was sad. I was scared at times, but I knew the One who went before me, and I trusted Him to fill me up in ways that only He could. He is so very good. Let Him love you today and give you the abundant life that only He can promise.

Lessons Learned

- When has it been hardest for you to trust the words of John 10:10?
- Why do you think it is difficult to remember Romans 8:5–6 when we are walking through suffering?
- How has God been your hope in the midst of the wilderness? If in a group setting, once everyone has shared a time in their lives or the life of someone around them, spend some time praising God for the wildernesses of life.

CHAPTER 26

THE POINT IS HIM

September 2014

*"Abba, into Your hands I entrust my body, mind, and spirit
and this entire day—morning, afternoon, evening, and night.
Whatever You want of me, I want of me, falling into You
and trusting in You in the midst of my life. Into Your heart I
entrust my heart, feeble, distracted, insecure, uncertain. Abba,
unto You I abandon myself in Jesus our Lord. Amen."*

—BRENNAN MANNING

GOALS. TO-DO LISTS. WE ALL have them. They look differently in each our
lives—some of them more planned out than others—but the most miserable among us is the one who is walking aimlessly around, without determining the purpose for which he or she lives. In some ways, this plays out
in our day-to-day living. Regardless, when death draws near, we all are
going to ask (if given the forewarning or chance): What did I do while I
was here? What was the purpose in it all?

September felt absolutely silent. There were test results pending
that would not come back for at least another month. Hugh was on the
night shift, which meant working at night and sleeping during the day.
It seemed like the days were filled with therapy, doctors' appointments,

home therapy, feeding, and then bed. Truthfully, in terms of milestones, we just weren't seeing much progress. Without knowing what to expect, it began to feel more and more mundane. I sometimes felt as if I was paddling around the same small lake, or pond really, over and over again, without any inkling that I was going to be getting out. This analogy became depressing to me during this season, as it felt so real. Even sadder, I realized the girls had only known this pond, and it felt like they had no idea that a huge river sat a few steps away.

I think part of the issue was how much I was viewing this whole thing with a goal-oriented mind-set, forgetting that the goal was not the choices we made or the decisions in the midst. The goal was always God Himself—more of Him and less of me. Here I was, feeling like I was in some small pond, when I had been in the rivers of God all along. In all things and all seasons, He had been leading me on in an adventure to Himself. The Word says this, "And whatever you do, in word or deed, do everything in the name of the Lord Jesus, giving thanks through Him to God the Father" (Colossians 3:17).

Whatever we do. Giving thanks through Him. You see, even our ability to thank Him in the midst came from Him and Him alone, for "from Him and through Him and for Him are all things" (Romans 11:36).

To some, these may seem like elementary truths. In some ways, yes they are. But really, this is the crux of the Gospel: that in all our seasons, in our questions, in our struggles, and in our joys, the goal is always more of Him. At the end of the day, in all our lives, the point is Him. How true it is that we would not know Him in the ways we do without all the pieces of the story He is writing. As I thought back on the past year and a half, and regardless of whether or not God chooses to heal our girls on this side of heaven or the next, I was positive that this whole thing had been worth it. It had been beautiful, both in our little family's life and in the kingdom. Beyond a shadow of a doubt, I knew that I would not know Him in the ways that I did had He not allowed our family to be rocked by this new normal. The purpose wasn't for me to be faithful in trusting until we got a diagnosis. It was not to begrudgingly walk through the day-to-day routine joyless but hopeful. No, the point was to be led closer and closer to an all-knowing, all-loving, active God who is always and forever up to something. May I never mistake His silence for lack of provision or lack of care. No, if He is being silent, rest assured that it is for purpose. He is doing something. Knowing that the goal is Him changes everything. It causes us to smile at whatever is in front or ahead, knowing that our hearts and minds should always be fixated on Him, the author and perfector of our faith (Hebrews 12:2). It reminds us, even in the mundane and in-betweens, that our purpose and our joy is still the same. Him.

So many people continued to say that Hugh and I must have had big faith to continue to praise God in this story, but I am here to say that I knew that was not the case. We did not have big faith, but we served a big God who was carrying us through it all. We are all told if we have faith as big as a mustard seed, then we can move mountains (Luke 17:6), but rest assured that power always comes from Him alone. We are given this ability because of Christ, by God's grace, and it is done through His Spirit and His doing, never our own.

Where does this leave you today? Friends, the goal is Him. Whether you are bogged down by the day-to-day routine or coasting through easy moments, He is it. He is the purpose in it all. As He leads us down His rivers of mercy, let's trust Him as the captain of our ship. Let's never mistake these rivers for our own little pond, for He is much, much bigger. We are grains of sand in His infinite beach. Yes, you are a grain of sand, but He knows your name, and He wants to give you the chance to know Him more deeply in all that today holds. We are not promised tomorrow. Let's look to Him as the one who truly brings purpose to our days. He is the goal. He is worthy. This truth made even the most scheduled days feel less mundane.

Lessons Learned

- Do you struggle with living from task to task and from goal to goal? Why do you think this is so tempting to do? What about living for goals is satisfying?
- Do you believe that the goal is always God Himself? If you trusted this more fully, how would your life look different?

CHAPTER 27

A BITTER SOUL

September 2014

"Give thanks in all circumstances; for this is the will of God in Christ Jesus for you."

—1 THESSALONIANS 5:18

BITTERNESS. IT SLOWLY CREEPS IN and has the tendency to poison the souls of both its victim and those closest. No one wants to think that they are angry; we would all love to consider ourselves a softened person, but when you look around, many of us carry resentment everywhere we go. At times, I knew that I was resembling more bitterness than tenderhearted trust. I knew God's truths. I read His promises and trusted that He was making all things new. But in the midst of the silence, I so often found my heart feeling very, very heavy. I knew His truth in my head but had a hard time transferring that to my heart. Jesus. His grace. I needed it-need it-so desperately.

By the end of September, about a year into our diagnosis search, I became exhausted by the roller coaster of my own emotions. I began to see so many similarities to the Israelites in our journey, however, and found such comfort that God calls Himself the God of the Israelites even in the midst of their wandering. Reading through the Old Testament, it is easy to think that surely the people of Israel would have learned from their past mistakes and not continued to sin against the Lord. I saw myself in those pages, and I hurt for them and for myself because I knew that each time we choose to trust in anything other than His sovereign goodness, we miss out in that moment. I am so grateful that He is working all things together for good. How thankful I am that the twists and turns in this life do not affect my ultimate destination: Him.

There was so much back and forth in the waiting. Some moments, I felt like a two-year-old child, beating her fists on the ground at the grocery store, begging for candy. Here I sat, at the feet of the Almighty, given full access, grumbling about the answers I thought I needed to find closure in our new normal. Complaining.

The Israelites were no different. In Exodus 14, God had literally provided for them through way of making the Red Sea dry in a split second. He destroyed the Egyptians in the sea, but, "...the people of Israel walked on dry ground through the sea, the waters being a wall to them on their right hand and on their left" (verse 29).

They rejoiced in God and His goodness immediately after, and, like many times before, seemed to be in a place of rest and trust. Not too far after that, they landed in the wilderness of Shur and were distressed because they could not find water there. They came to Marah, but they could not drink the water there because it was bitter: "And the people grumbled against Moses, saying, 'What shall we drink?'" (verse 24)

Don't miss that part, dear reader. They did not grumble to God. They complained to the one who He had sent to lead them. Ouch. How often did I lash out or express hurt to those around me, when truly my frustration was with the Lord and His current plan for my life? It probably seemed more appropriate to them to bring down Moses, but I bet if they were honest, their ultimate question was to their God. Was He really good? Was He really going to provide for them? Had He forgotten them? The last is a question that was asked in the Garden of Eden, and continues to be asked today.

There are days that the waiting, that the unknown, seemed bearable. On those days, I was truly able to rely on the Spirit to sustain me, and I was given the grace to trust despite the seeming silence. On others, I found myself bitter about where we were. I looked to those around me, mainly the ones who seemed to have things easier, and wondered why this had to be our lot. Distrust. I might have complained about the timeline, gotten upset with Hugh for not "getting me," but truly, I was discontent with the Lord's plans for us in those moments. I am no different than the Israelites. But God.

The Lord goes on to answer Moses's cries in the form of a log. Moses throws the log into the water, and the water becomes sweet. Afterward God exhorts the people to "diligently listen to the voice of the Lord your God, and do that which is right in His eyes, and give ear to His commandments and keep all His statutes..." (verse 26). He says if they will do this, He will put none of the diseases on them that He put on the Egyptians. Why? Because He is the Lord, their healer. Jehovah Rapha.

Think about the Egyptians. We have just read that they were all swallowed up by the Red Sea. The afflictions that truly brought them death were the afflictions of the heart. Friends, the ultimate healing balm we need is the healing of our own bitter souls. And while God used a log to turn the water sweet, this is not the only tree that has brought salvation. At Calvary, Jesus hung on the tree, bearing the weight of all our sin, in order to make our bitterness sweet. In all our moments, when we think of Jesus hanging there, the ultimate Hope that has been offered, all the things that we resent and feel angry toward are made right. He has taken all my bitterness and nailed it to the cross. Jesus. And, like the Israelites, although I will continue to stumble through this life—looking to His provision one second and cursing His plans the next—His sacrifice was enough, and He will safely carry me into eternity with Him. No more bitter tears.

Father, make us a people who trust You to be our Jehovah Rapha, in the waiting, in the hards, and in the moments that we cannot feel Your presence. Keep us beautifully connected to Your unchanging promises and help us to walk through this side of heaven with our eyes raised, fixed on you, not the circumstances that seem to overpower us. Nothing can defeat Your goodness. No one can alter Your plans for us, and they are good. In all our moments, both the bitter and the sweet, you are making all things new. What a precious and mighty God we serve! How grateful I was that He was continuing teach me these things, and that He continued to give me such undeserving grace even in my wanderings.

Lessons Learned

- Do you find yourself bitter or angry more often than not? At what or who?
- Read Exodus 14. Can you relate to the Israelites? Explain why or why not.
- How can trusting in God help us fight against grumbling?

CHAPTER 28

OUT

⌁

September 2014

"I will be with him in trouble, I will deliver him and honor him."

—Psalm 91:15

"Not always out of our troubled times, and the struggles fierce and grim, but in-deeper into our sure rest, the place of our peace, in Him."

—Annie Johnson Flint

As TIME WENT ON IN the waiting for answers, and as the girls' development seemed to be almost slowing in a sense, even recognition of the bitterness did not feel like enough. When I say enough, I mean that even understanding that God makes all bitter things sweet had not truly brought balm to my heart. I was restless. My soul was set firm on praising Him regardless, but my body and heart were weary. Toward the end of September, Hugh had been on a month of night shift. This meant even less help for me and not much sleep for him. I was essentially on day and night duty and had to fight for the joy to love our girls well. Weary.

As I tucked the girls into their cribs one night and sat down on the couch, an unfamiliar sensation hit me. Large, hot tears filled my eyes, and as I blinked them away, I realized how long it had been since I had cried. As I have said before, I tend to be a crier, but it seemed like in the in-between part of our journey, I kept those tears tucked deep inside. I knew the Lord would accept, collect, and use them. It was not His reaction that kept me from letting them flow; it was just that, if I was honest, I didn't even know where to start with processing where they would be coming from. Without a prognosis, without any sort of expectation, I didn't really know what to grieve. More on that later. Furthermore, if I was being authentic, I think I had been fearful if the tears started, I wouldn't be able to get them to stop. There was so much emotion bottled up inside of me, so many thoughts and pains.

I let the tears fall for just a minute, took a deep breath, wiped my eyes, and searched for a distraction in the form of the Internet. During this season, it was so refreshing to see life through the eyes of social media. At times, if things were just too hard, it was some sort of bandage for my aching heart. To read of others joys and hardships helped me to stay connected to a world that rejoices and mourns all at the same time. We all have those Band-Aids that we pull out from time to time. We will go there at some point too.

I turned on some praise and worship music, just searching for some comfort for the moment. As I pulled up my Facebook page, a friend of a friend had written a message to someone, and the words were exactly what I needed to read:

Wait

By: Russell Kelfer

Desperately, helplessly, longingly, I cried. Quietly, patiently, lovingly, He replied. I pleaded, and I wept for a clue to my fate, and the Master so gently said, "Child, you must wait."

"Wait? You say wait?" my indignant reply. "Lord, I need answers. I need to know why. Is your hand shortened? Or have you not heard? By faith I have asked, and I'm claiming your Word. My future, and all to which I can relate hangs in the balance, and you tell me 'wait'? I'm needing a 'yes,' a go-ahead sign, or even a 'no,' to which I can resign. And Lord, you have promised that if we believe, we need but ask, and we shall receive. And Lord I've been asking, and this is my cry: 'I'm weary of asking: I need a reply!'"

Then quietly, softly, I learned of my fate as my Master replied once again, "You must wait." So I slumped in my chair, defeated and taut and grumbled to God, "So I'm waiting, for what?"

He seemed then to kneel and His eyes met with mine and He tenderly said, "I could give you a sign. I could shake the heavens, darken the sun, raise the dead, and cause the mountains to run. All you see I could give, and pleased you would be. You would have what you want, but you wouldn't know Me. You'd not know the depth of my love for each saint; you'd not know the power that I give to the faint. You'd not learn to see through clouds of despair; you'd not learn to trust, just by knowing I'm there. You'd not know the joy of resting in Me, when darkness and silence was all you could see. You would never experience that fullness of love as the peace of my Spirit descends like a dove. You would know that I give, and I save, for a start, but you'd not know the depth of the beat of My heart. The glow of My comfort late in the night; the faith that I give when you walk without sight; the depth that's beyond getting just what you ask from an infinite God who makes what you have last. And you never would know, should your pain quickly flee, what it means that 'My grace is sufficient for thee.' Yes, your dreams for that loved one o'ernight could come true, but the loss! If you lost what I'm doing in you! So be silent, my child, and in time you will see that the greatest of gifts is to get to know Me. And though oft may My answers seem terribly late, My most precious answer of all…is still…wait."

These words pierced straight to my heart, and then, the words that I could not seem to express began to flow as freely as the tears that were streaming, "Lord, I am over this story. We have twins, both of them suffering from that which You will not reveal. It would be enough if one of them had something, but both of them? And, Father, I'm not even frustrated that You won't take it away. I trust there will be healing at some point, whether it is on this side of heaven or Yours, I just want to know what in the world it is, what we can expect going forward. Just a little break, God!" As the words literally left my heart and made their way to our living room, I felt Him gently whisper this truth: "Morgan, you say this side of heaven or Yours. My child, it is all mine. You know this. All things are being accomplished for my glory, and if it is for my glory, it will always be for your good. I knew that you would be faithful to praise my name in disease for your children. In order to grow you, I must stretch you farther than yourself. You are learning to give me praise in that which is most difficult for you: walking daily in the unknown."

In that moment, I understood. His discipline was truly out of love. When I say discipline, do not mistaken it for punishment. No, dear reader. This was not punishment in our lives. This was Him training me to know and love Him even more. And without this waiting, this growth could not occur. In His wisdom, He had known this all along. It's why He would allow something as rare as this to enter into our family's life: because without it, our love for Him would truly not be the same. For years, I had prayed to know Him more intimately, and here that prayer was being answered: His very best gift for us in this season. Friends, this is as true for me as it is for you. Whatever He has placed in your life, no matter how confusing or painful, He wants to use it to show more of Himself to you. So many people believe that a good God would not bring bad things to His children, and I could not agree more. You see, these things are not bad. If He has allowed them, they are His best for you, and He promises to use them to bring you to a deeper knowledge, understanding, and satisfaction in Him. Yes, even that.

As my heart began to accept this truth, and the tears became less frequent, my mind was brought to Romans 8:37: "No, in all these things we are more than conquerors through Him who loved us."

I have always focused on the "more than conquerors" and "through Him who loved us" part, but let's not miss the beginning: *in* all these things. In the verses prior, Paul listed many trials and tribulations that Christians had been walking through. God does not promise us that we would not walk through hard things, but He does assure us that in these things, He will make us victorious. In this world, we will have trouble, but take heart, dear friend. He has overcome the world (John 16:33).

While I still longed for answers, for direction, God was now bringing me to a place where I was less concerned about the answers and more concerned about knowing Him. Answers will never bring us satisfaction, but awareness and intimacy with our Creator always will. He is our peace. He was our ultimate Answer.

Lessons Learned

* What are your personal Band-Aids? If you have particular Band-Aids that you used to use but no longer do, why did you stop using them?
* Do you see discipline as love or as punishment? Why?
* Spend some time in God's Word, seeking out what God says will satisfy. If you are doing this in a group, spend some time reading some of these verses aloud together.

CHAPTER 29

LOVED AND CHERISHED

September 2014

"...The Lord appeared to him from far away. I have loved you with an everlasting love; therefore I have continued my faithfulness to you."

—JEREMIAH 31:3

MY GOD-FEARING, MANLIEST OF ALL men, hunk of a husband and I laid in bed one fall evening and talked about the challenges that came with taking care of our girls on a day-to-day basis.

"You know," I opened up to him, "it's not the taking care of them that's hard. It's all the therapies, appointments, expectations, and goals that wear on me, and them, I'm sure."

Hugh paused, thinking before he spoke (one of his strongpoints and one of my weaknesses), and said, "Babe, I think the most important thing we could ever do is make them feel loved and cherished each day. The world thinks so differently than that—the world thinks we should push them harder and focus on getting them stronger—but at the end of the day, I think God just calls us to show them His love. That's our goal." Loved and cherished. I thought a lot about that phrase in the days to come and felt such relief remembering that overall, that truly was what God had asked us to do. I thought back to those days past in which Hugh memorized

Psalm 139, in which we prayed that the girls would know God at a young age, and that they would understand His overwhelming, never-stopping love for them. Loved and cherished.

Bailey Grace and Ally Ruth. They were such content sixteen-month-olds. They lit up a room with their smiles and giggles; and they were not often found without a grin on their faces. When they cried, we took it seriously, as we knew that something was truly not right in their little world. They both loved music, being in the swimming pool, taking a bath, the Disney channel, books, and stroller walks. The girls would be content for hours, laying in their diapers, watching something on the television, or simply being smiled at or cuddled. These girls loved people in general, and they loved them to the best of their abilities. Ally's eyes lit up when you offered her blueberry yogurt; Bailey Grace prefered peaches or squash. I loved the predictable, gleeful look each of them gave when Hugh or myself picked them up and spins them around. They were truly beautiful on the inside and out.

At sixteen months, Ally Ruth and Bailey Grace were not sitting unassisted, whereas most all of their peers were walking with ease. They had difficulty using a pincher grasp, and while they loved playing with toys, their lack of appropriate fine motor skills made it challenging at times. The girls were not able to feed themselves and were not ready to eat more than baby food at that point. I continued to give them bottles, and keeping down the appropriate amount of calories did not always happen. Because they did not sit, if we were not at therapy, swimming, or in the stroller, the girls spent time in their high chairs, on their tummies, in their stander (a piece of therapeutic equipment), or in their exersaucers. Essentially, it was like we had pressed pause on a six-month developmental level, and we continued to live there. I reserved dinner time for what I had formally titled, "Diap and Disney time," in which they could lay on their backs in diapers, kick around, and just be free. They loved this part of the day, and I had grown to love it too because I knew they felt so content during it. Free to be Bailey Grace and Ally. Loved and cherished.

Isn't this what we all desire? To be free to be the souls God created us to be? To not have to worry about the expectations the world has put on each of us, and instead, just live the life God has prepared for us? I think back on those first few days with our precious girls—the days where I felt anxious about the idea of anyone ever saying one iota of a mean thing to my angels. The moments in which I felt like if everything in each of their little lives didn't go perfectly; I would crumble. I would have gone to the moon and back for my babies if that's what it took. I still would. The difference from the beginning to that point was that I had already spent sixteen months watching physicians and therapists analyze and overanalyze each and every move my beautiful girls had made. They spent most of their days being challenged to do things that, if we were honest, they may not have been made to do. This felt really hard to say, and I still get some negative responses to it. Many people felt like giving in to that mindset was failing to believe in our girls; beyond that, some people thought it was not having enough faith that God would heal them or that He had big plans for their lives. This all could not have been further from the truth. I am their momma. I, like other mommas, had dreamed about all the things my girls would do. I had thought about shopping dates, school dances, mother-daughter dinners, and even planning their weddings together. I had pondered the girls growing up and what that would look like. Would they go to college together or separately? What career path would they choose? What activities would they be passionate about? Tears sting my eyes as I type this because here is the truth: our current reality just didn't lend true to most of these things happening. My expectations had to be lowered; and at that point, I simply longed for the day I heard, "I love you momma." That would be enough.

I believed that God could do that which He chose at any and all times. He is sovereign over all, and His ways are good. He has healed before, and He could do so in our lives in an instant. But here's the thing: this journey had taken me to a level of intimacy with our God that I had never even touched. I knew more than ever before that I was loved, and I had fallen more in love with Him than I ever knew possible. In light of those things, it was also very clear to me that His ways were not our ways. Sometimes His plans do not include healing on this side of heaven, not in spite of His goodness but because of His goodness. I wanted what He wanted. I desired that which brought Him glory, and if not healing Ally and Bailey Grace while they are on earth was His best, the Spirit inside me wanted that wholeheartedly.

Many people do not believe that God is in control of disease, sickness, and hardship. Even well-meaning Christians will say that a good God would not allow bad things. Here's the thing: If that was true, then that means that God is not in control of this earth. And if He isn't in control, then He isn't sovereign. If He isn't sovereign, then is He really worth worshipping or trusting? No. My God is in absolute control of every detail that goes on, both on this side of earth and the next. He is working all things together for good, and what we may consider bad is yet another thread in His perfect kingdom. This I knew to be true: Ally and Bailey Grace would be healed. We all will. When we meet Him face-to-face, He is going to show us the healing that He already earned for us on the cross. You see, healing has already occurred. We may not have seen it then, but it doesn't make it any less true.

The Bible says,

So we do not lose heart. Though our outer self is washing away, our inner self is being renewed day by day. For this light momentary affliction is preparing for us an eternal weight of glory beyond all comparison, as we look not to the things that are seen but to the things that are unseen. For the things that are seen are transient, but the things that are unseen are eternal" (2 Corinthians 4:16–18).

Don't you see? It is all light and momentary. Today it may feel like a house full of bricks on your shoulders, but in the big scheme of things, it is a feather. We are all vapor. The Word of God says that we do not know what tomorrow will bring because "you are a mist that appears for a little time and then vanishes" (James 4:14). That is all any of us has on this earth. Whether we are the infant that passes away before he or she takes his or her first breath or the one-hundred-year-old great-grandmother who dies peacefully in her sleep, all is dust. This is why we can accept whatever His loving hand brought us: we can be confident that it is passing. Our life on earth does not last long. We can either spend our time living for the temporary, which is here today and gone tomorrow, or we can invest in that which will never fade, namely Jesus. Belief in Christ and what He did for us on the cross gives us the freedom to take the easy days and the hard days in the same way. We can accept all things as loving gifts from His hand, knowing that if He died for our sins, we can certainly trust Him with today and all it holds. If He was able to nail death to the cross and pronounce victory over that which held all of us done, can He not give us the strength to walk through any and all circumstances? His Word makes it clear that in this world, we will have many troubles, but that we can take heart, knowing He has already overcome the world (John 16:33). Jesus.

Back to being loved and cherished. I was not suggesting that we stop therapy with the girls or that any of us just frolic around in fields, doing whatever we want, waiting for Jesus to come back. No. We do live in this world for now, and there are things that God has called us to do while we are here. What I was suggesting, however, is that we challenge ourselves to take on an attitude of accepting people where they are. This even applies to our personal walks with the Lord. I have found that many times, I am guilty of wanting someone to be at a level of sanctification that I desire for them. Not only is this arrogant, it is also not trusting in God's journey for that individual. Sure we are all called to pursue holiness (Hebrews 12:14). We are taught to seek the Lord and His standards in all things. However, we are also assured that we are still in our flesh and that we will not reach His perfection on this side of heaven. This is why Jesus came in the first place! He gave His righteousness for our rags. So while we seek holiness, while we desire to be more like Him, we also must learn to give others (and ourselves) the grace that He has offered us. If Jesus's death on the cross was enough for God to forgive, how dare we set a different standard.

We must never cease to meet people where they are. We are all messy, imperfect human beings. We struggle with different things—our journeys are not the same—but we can connect on the level that until we leave this earth, we will be human. This is the plan that God Himself set up. Knowing that, we must continue to seek to love others in that way. To look at His word, the way that He chose to do things in all His wisdom, and allow Him to pursue the hearts of others through the vapor He has given us.

When I sought to love our girls without striving to make them anything but who God created them to be, I was blessed. The days that I did not stress out about their performance or milestones were the days that we all smiled more. When I trie to fight the way that God created Ally and Bailey Grace to be, I was fighting against the hand of God. I wanted to choose to accept the way that He made them—perfectly, in His image, yesterday, this day, and tomorrow. Friends, this is true for each of us. Whether we are trying to make ourselves or those around us different, we must throw up our white flags and realize it is not up to us to choose that which God has created. If we reach peoples' hearts, it will not be because we have pushed them to be something they are not. It will be because God's Spirit has pierced them to the core in light of the fact that He accepts them exactly where they are.

As it says in the Bible, "But God shows His love for us in that while we were still sinners, Christ died for us" (Romans 5:8).

Two verses before, it says, "For while we were still weak, at the right time" (Romans 5:6). Don't you see? Praise God He doesn't wait for me to get it together to embrace me. Thank You, Lord, that You chose me in my weakness and that You loved me just as I am.

Friends, he loves you as you are. He loves the people He has placed in your life as they are. Yes, because He loves us, He wants us to pursue righteousness and not death. Out of His love, through Jesus, He gave us a way to pursue that which brings us life. Let's not confuse sanctification with conditional love. No. You are unconditionally loved and cherished. My prayer for each of us is that, like Bailey Grace and Ally during "Diap and Disney Time," we would abandon the constraints the world tries to put on us and run to the freedom that is offered through the love of Christ, eternally loved and cherished. I had slowly begun to understand that disability, diagnosis or not, could never take away the main calling God had placed on our lives as parents: to love Ally and Bailey Grace with a love that knew no boundaries and to point them to the One who loved them from before the beginning of time.

Lessons Learned

* Who makes you feel most loved and cherished? Why?
* Do you struggle with thinking that your acceptance is directly correlated to your performance? If so, explain how and why you think that is.
* What does God's word say about our acceptance? Where does God say our acceptance is found?
* How can you practically love and cherish those around you in the ways God has called you to do so? If in a group, spend some time discussing particular ways you could love one another well in the coming week.

CHAPTER 30

HIS WILL, HIS WAY

"For my thoughts are not your thoughts, neither are your ways my ways, declares the Lord. For as the heavens are higher than the earth, so are my ways higher than your ways and my thoughts than your thoughts."

—ISAIAH 55:8–9

"For everything there is a season, and a time for every matter under heaven..."

—ECCLESIASTES 3:1A

"Yet you are holy."

—PSALM 22:3A

IT IS WINTER NOW, AND I am sitting in a local coffee shop, sipping on a Gingerbread latte and enjoying the beauty of the colder months. I tend to love the change of the seasons, but in ways, this one tastes a little bittersweet.

When I began writing this book, I wrote it in full expectation of ending it with a diagnosis. I planned on telling you that I got the answers and then explaining how God had led me to a place where I didn't need answers anymore, but I just needed Him. Like a movie with a surprising twist, God continues to work in my heart and remind me that His story, His merciful pen, does not write like my own. Hugh and I traveled to the National Institute of Health with the girls in order to participate in their Undiagnosed Disease Program. I was sure there would be absolutely no way we would not leave without direction. Again, I was left wanting. For a couple of months, I hit a block in which I was not sure what else there was to say or where else there was to go. The words did not seem to flow; and the lessons felt much more blurry. What I have finally realized is that truly, the only thing I have to offer anyone is the beauty of the journey that He has created. The truth is that the goal of this story, of all our stories, is Him. Through all the highs and lows of this life, He continues to pursue. I, like the Israelites, have been on a roller coaster in which I trust God one second and become suspicious of His love the next. Many books simply show a person's strong faith throughout their particular journey; this is clearly not one of those books. My love for Him has swayed, but one thing has remained: He is relentless in His love for us. No matter where I have been in it all, no matter where I continue to go, He has a hold of me and is not letting go. His faithfulness lingers above all else. Our journey with our beautiful, fearfully and wonderfully made, precious baby girls has looked different than other seasons of our life, but the purpose has still been the same: more of Him and less of me. The one thing that stands sure is that with or without a diagnosis, He will always be the center of this story. The miracle in our family's life continues to be that through it all, His hand stays firm and He is knitting the details of our lives together, walking us from glory to glory in ways that only He can do.

"And we all, with unveiled face, beholding the glory of the Lord, are being transformed into the same image from one degree of glory to another. Or this comes from the Lord who is the Spirit."

—2 Corinthians 3:18From one degree of glory to another. Here lies the crux of all of our lives. That truth encompasses the beautiful picture of His protecting, intentional love that began not at the cross, but from the beginning. You see, this was His plan all along. Jesus was not plan B.

He was God's determination to save a broken and sinful world since before time as we know it. The circumstances, struggles, and triumphs of our individual lives may be completely different, but at the end of the day, His goal for each of us remains the same. He is bringing beauty from the ashes of all of our hards, and His love will carry us from glory to glory until we meet Him face-to-face. There is no greater joy than this.

I may not be in those newborn trenches anymore, but I pray that I stay firm in the trenches of God's glorious story. I pray that, while I may stumble, I continually make my way back to the God who has never failed and never will, to the God who has walked me through this unimaginable journey thus far. The same God who walked the road to Calvary, who rescued me and captured my heart for all eternity by taking on all my sin and shedding His own blood, is working in all these things for good. We cannot ever lose sight of His sovereign place in this journey. My prayer for you, dear reader, is the same. It is my hope and prayer that God has used the pages of this book to open your heart and soul to more of His glory and light in your own life and that, while different, you might have connected to the goodness of God in all our stories. I pray that the land of Milk and Honey that He has led us to has directed your heart toward Him in whatever season or place He has you in. You see, this story is not about me, Hugh, Ally, or Bailey Grace; it's about Him. Diagnosis or not, His glory remains. Through sweat, blood, and tears, may we fight to hold fast to Him. I can promise you this: He's not letting go of you. He is not dropping Mercy's pen for even a second in your story or mine. He's got this. And one day, He will come and bind together each of our pages, all the chapters of all the journeys of all His children, into one big, glorious book. And all, with unveiled faces, will fall at the feet of Jesus, stories no longer in our minds, as we worship Him forever.

Lessons Learned

* Do you see God pursuing you in the highs and lows of every season? What piece of your journey currently feels like your own version of the land of Milk and Honey? Why?
* What is a truth about Jesus that you did not grasp prior to reading this book, but you do now?
* Moving forward, how can you continue to look for God in all the pieces of the story He is writing in your life? How can you encourage others around you to do the same? If in a group, discuss particular ways you want to be kept accountable in this area.

REFERENCES

All Scripture quotations, unless otherwise noted, are taken from the Holy Bible, English Standard Version.

Chapter 1
Lewis, C.S. The Four Loves (San Diego: Harcourt, Inc., 1960), 169-170.

Chapter 3
Manning, Brennan. The Relentless Tenderness of Jesus (Ada: Fleming H. Revell, 2004), 68.

Chapter 5
Story, Laura. What if Your Blessings Come Through Raindrops- A 30 Day Devotional (Brentwood: Freeman-Smith, 2012), 162.

Chapter 6
Story, Laura. What if Your Blessings Come Through Raindrops- A 30 Day Devotional (Brentwood: Freeman-Smith, 2012), 80.

Chapter 7
Lewis, C.S. The Essential C.S. Lewis ed. Dorsett, Lyle (New York: Simon and Schuster, 1996), 362.

Chapter 9
Liddell, Karni. "A Happy Baby." YouTube video, 16:38, January 27, 2014, https://www.youtube.com/watch?v=GFTeBdp__Rg.

Lewis, C.S. The Essential C.S. Lewis ed. Dorsett, Lyle (New York: Simon and Schuster, 1996), 93.

Chapter 14
Spurgeon, Charles. The Treasury of David: Containing an Original Exposition of the Book of Psalms Vol. 7 (New York: I.K. Funk and Company, 1886), 68.

Chapter 19
Cowman, L.B. Streams in the Desert ed. Reimann, Jim (Grand Rapids: Zondervan, 2008 edition), 194.

Chapter 21
Platt, David. Radical: Taking Back Your Faith from the American Dream (Colorado Springs: Multnomah Books, 2010), 181.

Chapter 22
Story, Laura. What if Your Blessings Come Through Raindrops- A 30 Day Devotional (Brentwood: Freeman-Smith, 2012), 176.
Williams, Pharrell. Despicable Me. *Despicable Me: Original Motion Picture Soundtrack.* (Santa Monica: Interscope/Pharrell, 2010).

Chapter 23
Cowman, L.B. Streams in the Desert ed. Reimann, Jim (Grand Rapids: Zondervan, 1997 edition), 157.
Voskamp, Ann. One Thousand Gifts (Grand Rapids: Zondervan, 2010), 20-21.

Chapter 25
Cowman, L.B. Streams in the Desert ed. Reimann, Jim (Grand Rapids: Zondervan, 1997 edition), 315.

Chapter 26
Manning, Brennan. Ruthless Trust: The Ragamuffin's Path to God (Grand Rapids: Zondervan, 2002), 11.

Chapter 28
Cowman, L.B. Streams in the Desert ed. Reimann, Jim (Grand Rapids: Zondervan, 1997 edition), 341.
Pickering, J. Ben. Talking with God: Discovering Prayer (Melbourne, Australia: Zenan Media and Publishing, 2014), 159-160.

Morgan would be honored if you would continue to follow the story God is writing in the Cheeks' lives at hishandshisfeethisheart.com.

ABOUT THE AUTHOR

Morgan Cheek is a licensed social worker, public speaker, and stay-at-home mom to Ally and Bailey Grace—two wonderfully, uniquely, and differently abled twin girls. She currently resides in Birmingham, Alabama, with her husband, Hugh, who recently finished his pediatric residency. Cheek is the author of "His Hands, His Feet, His Heart," a Christian blog with a focus on the journey to seeing God in all things.

Made in the USA
San Bernardino, CA
23 November 2015

26180197R00110